With Sunshine Comes Shadow

Beverley Scott

Copyright © 2023 Beverley Scott

All rights reserved.

ISBN: 9798852621627

DEDICATION

THIS BOOK IS DEDICATED TO MY FAMILY.

CONTENTS

Chapter 1

Chapter 2

Chapter 3

Chapter 4

Chapter 5

Chapter 6

Chapter 7

Chapter 8

Chapter 9

Chapter 10

Chapter 11

Chapter 12

Chapter 13

Chapter 14

Chapter 15

Chapter 16

Chapter 17

Chapter 18

Chapter 19

Chapter 20

Chapter 21

Chapter 22

Chapter 23

Chapter 24

Chapter 25

Chapter 26

Chapter 27

Chapter 28

Chapter 29

Chapter 30

Chapter 31

Chapter 32

Chapter 33

CHAPTER 1

Joy and woe are woven fine,
A clothing for the soul divine.
Under every grief and pine,
Runs a joy with silken twine.

William Blake

Port Elizabeth - 27 June 1981

Our wedding in the church hall was a small but rather jolly affair, officiated by a young magistrate, in front of close family members and friends. After the civil marriage ceremony the bottles of sparkling wine were popped, snacks were brought to the tables, a short speech was made, a song was sung, and then we all got down to celebrating.

Patrick and I had known each other for several years, but only as casual acquaintances. He was a student at the Law Faculty of the University of Port Elizabeth, and he attended the same lectures as my brother and then husband. Together with a few other fellow students, Patrick very often came over to our place for drinks and a fair bit of partying, so naturally we saw each other in that context. It was only after my marriage ended and I became single that we got to know each other well enough, and eventually we developed a relationship. As things stood then, not everyone thought it was a good idea for Patrick to get involved with a divorcee, and mother of two small children, especially since he was still a student. But the doubters were very much in the minority, and most of our friends and family seemed happy for us when we decided to get married. On the day of our marriage we couldn't afford an official photographer, so we handed my small Kodak camera to my younger brother Clive and asked him to take the wedding photos for us. He did his best with my tiny camera, but ultimately the day was saved when a good friend, who also happened to be an excellent photographer, appeared with his camera equipment. "I thought you might like a few photos", he tactfully offered, and a week or so later, much to our delight, he presented us with a set of beautiful wedding photos. Of course, we also had quite a lot of tiny, rather blurry, snaps taken by my brother on the Kodak camera, and they sit proudly in our wedding album with the other photos, as a reminder of how little money we had all those years ago, when we got married.

After our marriage Patrick took on the role of stepfather to my two boys, six-year-old Alex and four-year-old Derrick, and despite living on a shoestring, in a small flat, we all settled into the new family dynamic and living arrangement very quickly and naturally. For the first two years of our marriage Patrick was still a student and we were very grateful to receive financial assistance from my parents, although we still did odd jobs to supplement our income and make ends meet. One of the jobs was very odd indeed – we had to park our car at the entrance of a large shopping complex and count the cars entering and leaving. We used to park our little VW Golf at the entrance and spend several hours counting cars, with two very energetic and rather bored little boys bouncing around the hot and stuffy car. Even now, I can't think why any company would pay someone to do that, but we got paid by the hour, so we didn't care about the reasons. We were just happy about the money.

We lived a very frugal life for several years, during which Patrick graduated, and then did his compulsory military service, which he did as a legal advisor for the South African Prisons Service for four years. After military service, he completed his pupilage and gradually built up his legal practice as a very successful advocate. Meanwhile, I had a steady flow of piano pupils over the years, working mostly from home as our family grew, first with another son, and many years later, a daughter.

Our son William was five years old when Patrick finally started his practice as an advocate, and one evening Patrick said to him, "Now that Daddy has a decent job, if you had to choose something, what would to like me to buy for you?"

Without hesitation William replied, "I would like real shoes please Daddy".

Until then he had only ever had canvas trainers, not proper leather shoes, and they were often third hand, having been worn first by Alex and then by Derrick. Needless to say, his next pair of shoes were his very own new, "real" leather shoes, and he was ever so proud of them.

CHAPTER 2

It was clear from an early age that Alex was a born performer and mimic, and one of his favourite programs on the radio was 'The Goon Show'. He used to record each episode on his little tape recorder and listen to the shows over and over, until he knew every single episode off by heart. By the age of eight he could do very good renditions of the Goons, perfectly imitating Neddy Seagoon, Captain Bloodnok, Eccles, Bluebottle, Moriarty, and others. Alex loved comedy and mimicry, and he kept us endlessly entertained with his antics. He was also a huge fan of Spike Milligan, and he could perform a very funny rendition of the song 'Ying Tong Iddle I Po', or recite various poems written by Spike Milligan. In many ways his peers at primary school quite simply didn't understand his sense of humour or his quirky take on life. Very few, if any, of them even knew who Spike Milligan was, let alone 'The Goon Show'. But at home Alex was fortunate to have access to Patrick's large collection of Spike Milligan books, including his poems, because Patrick had been a huge fan of Spike Milligan for many years, and that shared interest between them remained firm over the years.

As Alex grew older, he learned to play the trumpet, and by the time he was fifteen he was playing in a professional jazz band every Saturday afternoon. As a young White boy living in Apartheid South Africa, this was strictly speaking not permitted. In South Africa, Whites were not allowed into areas which were classified as "Black" or "Coloured". Just as there were curfew laws to curtail the access of anyone other than White people to "White" areas after dark. However,

Alex was undaunted, as were Patrick and I, and much as we may have been subject to the Apartheid laws of the time, that did not mean we were going to bow down to them unless we had absolutely no choice. The only clubs that featured jazz musicians were in so-called "non-White" areas, and as a budding jazz trumpeter Alex went where the music was, which meant we would have to transport him to the venues when he performed. He very quickly became known as a sensational young jazz musician, for his talent as well as for being the only "Whitey", as he was fondly called by the other musicians, and by the time he left school at the age of eighteen, he was playing with very well-known and famous South African jazz musicians. He eventually settled in Cape Town, where his prospects were much better than they were in Port Elizabeth, although life as a musician, or any artist, is hard wherever they may be, and it was a struggle for him to earn a decent income. Despite this, he followed his star regardless of the hardships, although he did occasionally ask me to bail him out when he couldn't pay his rent. It took several years of really difficult times and sheer determination, but he built up a very good reputation in the music circles of Cape Town and the surrounding areas, and with time his reputation spread much further afield, mainly to Stockholm and Basel.

As a professional musician, Alex travelled around a great deal. It was a standing joke between him and me that he did not need a permanent place to live, all he needed was a rented locker at the airport. But no matter how often he was on the road, or abroad, he would always let me know where he was going and what he was doing, and in the summer of 2003 I received an email from him telling me that he was working as a waiter on the Isle of Arran, because he was hoping to supplement his insecure income. It is an unfortunate truth that as much as people love to have music in their lives, they are very reluctant to pay the musicians a decent rate, and for Alex this was the reality, which meant he had to try and earn extra money in other ways from time to time. In his emails from the Isle of Arran he had many tales to tell about the beautiful place and the interesting people. He told me of the standing stones on Machrie Moor and of the wonderful mountains, which he found very inspiring, and he often tried to trick me with Gaelic words which he learned from an elderly lady who came into the tearoom every day. But I always outfoxed him by looking up the meaning online and pretending that I knew Gaelic, and he never caught me out on my little secret.

Since I had never heard of the Isle of Arran, I was curious to know where it was, so I consulted our large map of the UK to see if I could locate it. When I finally found it, I saw that it was not much more than a pinprick on the large map, sitting off the west coast of Scotland. Ultimately though, I didn't think too much about it, because I saw it as just another far-flung place where he happened to be, albeit rather different from the usual places he went to. When I mentioned to Patrick that Alex was working on a small island called the Isle of Arran, he had the same reaction as me - he was interested to hear where Alex was, but he had never heard of the place either, and we didn't think about it again for a very long time.

Derrick was far more interested in insects and animals than anything else, and he always had a very good connection with nature. It will probably be quite accurate to describe him as an 'animal whisperer' because he always seems totally connected to all creatures. As a very small boy he used to keep one or two pet snails in a big bottle, but as he grew a bit older his fascination with nature did not stop with snails, and this led to a few not so pleasant encounters, such as the occasions when he brought weird, and sometimes downright scary, little creatures from school in his school case. For him, schoolbooks were less important than taking a closer look at nature, and he spent many hours observing the minutest insects in the garden at home or the playground at school. That was all good and well, until he started to bring creatures back from school, causing some rather hair-raising moments.

One day he arrived at the car after school and announced that he had a big lizard in his school case. He even showed me his finger, which was sporting a nasty bite, and informed me that the lizard had bitten him.

"How big is that lizard?" I asked, eyeing him with suspicion.

"It's the biggest lizard I have ever seen", he said proudly.

"Well you will have to let it go. Take it back to where you found it", I insisted. After all, I was the parent, and I knew best, didn't I?

Of course I knew best, but he pleaded loudly and tearfully with me to let him take it home to our garden, and despite my reservations I gave in and allowed him to keep the lizard, adding one very big proviso - he was not allowed to open his school case until we were at home and out of the car. With his earnest promise that he would keep his school case closed I drove off.

We were almost halfway home when a small voice from the back of the car said, "Oh no, the lizard has escaped".

I almost ran the car off the road as I yelled at him in horror, "What do you mean the lizard escaped, you were not supposed to open the case!"

"But I just opened the suitcase to peep in", he replied, clutching his case to his chest.

It would be a massive understatement to say that the rest of the drive home was not very pleasant, because I kept imagining a big fat lizard crawling onto my foot, or up my leg. By the time we got home I was absolutely fuming, but there was not much point in going on about it because the darned lizard was already lurking in my car, and I would have to get it out. I decided to leave all the car doors and the boot open, I removed as much of the carpeting as possible, and then I just hoped for the best that the lizard would make a dash for freedom. But how would I know if it had? Or hadn't? I could only hope it would escape into the garden, because sooner or later I would have to use the car, and I did not appreciate the possibility that I may have a resident lizard onboard.

The moment for me to get into the car came later that afternoon when I had to set off for the supermarket to do the daily grocery shopping. My car had been left with doors and boot open for several hours, but I had no idea what the lizard had done about escaping into the garden, so with my fingers crossed and with my skin crawling at the thought, I closed the boot and the doors, got in my seat, fastened my seatbelt, and started the car. And then I saw it. Derrick was right when he said it was the biggest lizard he had ever seen. And now that big, fat lizard was watching me with steely eyes from the steering wheel shaft, barely twelve inches away from my face. With a shriek, I was out of the car quicker than a flash of lightning, shouting for Derrick to get himself outside immediately, and to get the darned thing out of my car. The lizard was duly released into the garden and the episode was more or less forgotten. Until he brought his next "friend" home. And the only positive thing about this particular episode was that the creature in question did not escape into the car, because I fear I would have torched my car rather than get into it ever again!

He brought a huge spider home in his school case, keeping very quiet about his stowaway, probably because he knew I would not allow him to bring it near my car, let alone *in* my car. At least he had learned the lesson about "opening my suitcase to peep in", and I was blissfully unaware of our unwanted passenger until the boys had finished their lunch, and he called me to come and see the huge spider. The menacing looking creature was on the carpet, and it was slowly but determinedly heading my way. I leapt onto a chair in horror, yelling at him to get rid of it. But it was very large, very ugly, and very unstoppable, and even Derrick said he wasn't too keen on having it in the house after all, which didn't help much since it was already there, and it certainly didn't look like the kind of spider that could be caught in a jar. I screamed at him for bringing it home, he stood on the bed and yelled that he didn't like the spider, and a general sense of bedlam ensued, as the spider crawled towards us. Eventually I had to leap off the chair and deal with the problem, and I decided to dispatch the spider into eternity with a large rock. I can't say I am proud of my action, but a desperate situation called for a desperate solution, and the young nature-loving spider catcher was not too keen to deal with it, so it was up to me to do what I thought was best.

Needless to say, after that debacle I issued a serious warning of dire consequences if any form of nature was brought into the house without my permission.

"Not even a leaf!" I warned him. And thankfully that was the last time he brought any living creatures home from school. He never lost his curiosity in nature, but he confined his discoveries to our garden.

Since we already had a ready-made family when we were married, and Patrick also wanted a child of his own, we started discussing having a baby a few months after our marriage. We thought it would be better to raise the children together while they were all still young.

Alex was eight years old, and Derrick was six, when our son William was born. He was an easy-going baby and Alex was completely smitten by his baby brother from the very first moment he saw him. The day we brought the newborn William home Alex practically cartwheeled around the flat he was so excited, and he fussed over his baby brother all the time. As William grew older into toddlerhood, Alex was like a mother hen, keeping a watchful eye over him. He taught William to play chess when he was only three years old, and he also took great pride in sharing his Goon Show recordings with William, as well as teaching him Spike Milligan poems. They had an extremely close bond throughout their lives; so close that at times it seemed they were telepathically connected.

When William was about eighteen years old he was working in a shop inside a large shopping mall, and he had the terrifying experience of being caught in the crossfire of an armed robbery. Within minutes of the shootout stopping, William received a text message from Alex, who was in Sweden at the time: "William, are you okay? What is happening?" Even at that distance, completely separated from his little brother, Alex knew William was in danger, and he reached out to him.

William was a very intelligent child who loved reading. It was fortunate that he had a large collection of books thanks to his two older brothers, because he worked his way through books at a phenomenal speed. When he was about six years old I asked him what job he wanted to do when he grew up, and he told me he was going to be a reader. I asked him what a reader would do as a career, and he replied, "If I am a reader I will read, of course".

As he grew older, and as the world of computer technology became much more accessible to everyone, he decided his future career would be in that direction. Courses in computer technology were not as common during the late 1990's as they are nowadays, but when he was about fifteen years old we managed to enroll him in an extra-curricular computer course at a local high school where classes were offered during the afternoons. William had found his niche, and it was a foregone conclusion that he would follow a career in computer technology. After finishing school he studied an intensive one-year course at the Computer Training Institute, or CTI, and a few months after he graduated he was offered a position at CTI as a tutor, where he worked for some time until they transferred him from Port Elizabeth to Johannesburg. He had always been very focused and ambitious, and within less than two years he had established himself as a valuable employee at CTI, and he had bought himself a new car and his own home in a gated community. At the same time, he continued to study, always expanding his knowledge and expertise, by continually adding to his qualifications. He would go on to add two more degrees to his achievements, and even after that he planned to enroll for more qualifications. It seemed that he was "a reader" after all.

As far as we were concerned our family was complete with our three boys. But life has a way of changing thoughts and minds, and at a time in our lives when it should have been an unlikely topic to consider, we were talking about trying our luck in the hopes of having a daughter. We were comfortably settled in our lifestyle, and having a baby in the home again was not something we had thought about until then, but sometimes it is wise to ignore what seems sensible or rational and to just take a leap of faith. That is precisely what we did, and our daughter Catherine was born in 1994, when Alex was twenty, Derrick was eighteen and William was almost twelve. Most of our friends believed it was an unplanned pregnancy and we had a good few 'nudge, nudge, wink, wink' comments, but they were wrong, and we never missed the opportunity to enlighten them about their mistaken thinking. She was very much planned, and we were delighted to have a daughter.

It was not all plain sailing though, as the pregnancy was fraught with difficulties, and there was a constant risk that I may not carry the baby to full term. Everything was medically managed every step of the way, including the daily taking of drugs, bi-weekly injections for the first few months, and ultimately a two-week hospital stay on a drip, which fell over the Christmas period of 1993. It was a rather miserable time, but I knew that every day closer to the delivery date meant less risk for the unborn baby. One morning Patrick arrived with a bag of Christmas tinsel to jolly up my drip stand, and for Christmas that year he gave me a large mug bearing the words: "I'd rather be forty than pregnant", much to the amusement of the nursing staff. Especially since I was both!

After the long months of anxiety and stress our daughter was born two weeks before the due date, weighing in at just over 4 kilograms, or 9 pounds, alert and determined to take on the world. Having a little girl in the family was like the proverbial icing on the cake, and just as Alex had fallen in love with his baby brother in 1982, William was completely enamoured by his baby sister. The two older boys were no longer living at home, and William became my second pair of hands, always willing to push her in her pram, pacify her, entertain her, and cuddle her. And as she grew older, he was always at hand to watch over her. He was extremely protective of his sister, and they were very close, despite the almost twelve-year difference in their ages.

As a small child Catherine was an observer and collector of insects, very much like Derrick used to be, and her huge, beautifully furnished doll house didn't have a single doll occupant. Instead, it was home to snails and bugs, which she housed in an unused fish tank when they were not "playing" in the doll house. She was also very talented at drawing from an extremely early age, and it was fortunate that Patrick always had a large supply of usable A4 scrap paper from his workplace, because she spent a lot of time drawing. She never ran out of ideas, and she would easily fill twenty or more pages a day drawing pictures. When she was a teenager we gave her carte blanche to decorate her bedroom walls and she filled the walls with murals from corner to corner. Fortunately her bedroom was very large, with high ceilings, so she had more than enough space to exercise her artistic talent, although occasionally her ideas where a bit odd, such as when she asked us to have her ceiling and two of the walls painted black. It was a very high ceiling and she said she wanted to try and counter the height by having it painted black. We had our reservations, but we asked our regular painter to come and do the job for us, and the look on his face was nothing less than incredulous.

"Pottie, we want you to paint the ceiling black", I said.
"No, no, it can't be black", he insisted.
"Yes, it has to be black", I repeated.
"No, it can't be black", was his steadfast reply.

The debate went around in circles for quite some time, until I eventually won him over, but he just shook his head, gave a low whistle, and laughed softly, probably thinking we had lost our minds. He did the job, and the final result looked a lot better than we expected, with him eventually conceding that it wasn't bad at all. He did paintwork for us for many years, and we often had a good laugh together about that conversation, and the black ceiling and walls.

CHAPTER 3

It is the hope of every parent that all their children will live happy, healthy, and meaningful lives, and it is a rare parent who in the deepest part of their heart doesn't fear that one of their children may come to harm. We care for them and nurture them until they leave the nest, and then we have to trust that they will be safe in the big world. But unfortunately that is not always the case.

For our family everything changed on 7 January 2009, when Alex died tragically in a car crash near Cape Town. He was living in a flat in Strand, outside Cape Town, and he had been working as the music director on a wine farm near Franschhoek since 2007. When he started his work on the wine farm, he told me that he felt he had finally found the job of his dreams. Being a professional musician meant a steady income was never guaranteed, and he used to travel to Europe frequently to earn extra money, because in South Africa he did not earn enough to be financially secure. His new job as music director offered him the security of a good income and a wonderful opportunity to research indigenous South African music. He was also appointed to train and direct the brass band on the farm, of which all the members were farm workers or children of farm workers. He was positively glowing whenever he told us about his new job and his new responsibilities, and we were really happy that he had finally found his niche and that he could look forward to a positive future, in a job he loved.

As we approached the end of 2008, Patrick and I were discussing our plans for the Christmas holidays, and we decided that we would spend Christmas at our holiday home near Knysna, which is on the Garden Route. I phoned Alex and asked him if he could join us there for Christmas because William would be flying down from Johannesburg to spend Christmas and New Year with us. Alex was very keen, but he told me that he would have to leave early on Boxing Day because he had a performance on the evening of 26 December, in Franschhoek. That put us in a quandary, because as much as we wanted him to spend Christmas with us, we were worried about him travelling from Knysna back to Cape Town, a four-hour journey, on Boxing Day. Road fatalities in South Africa are very high at the best of times, but over the Christmas period the statistics are quite horrific, with alcohol playing a large part in the high rate of traffic accidents. Having Alex on the road at that time was too worrying, so we changed our plans. We decided to spend Christmas in Cape Town, in our holiday flat, which meant we were in the same city, and Alex would not have to risk the dangerous roads. And as a bonus, Alex said he would arrange tickets for us to his performance in Franschhoek on the evening of 26 December.

As she often did, Catherine had brought a friend on holiday with her for company, and while Patrick and I were preparing Christmas lunch in the kitchen on Christmas Day, we could hear Alex in his usual form, causing outrageous bursts of laughter with his antics. Having Spike Milligan as his childhood idol truly rubbed off on him, because he turned everything into a comedic sketch, and we often laughed until our sides ached when he was with us. It was a family joke that his laughter could set a flock of birds to flight.

Over lunch we enjoyed a few bottles of the sparkling wine, 'Cape Jazz Shiraz', which Alex had brought for us from the wine farm. He told us he was very chuffed with the wine as well as the label, which reinforced the role that music played on the wine farm, and he spent a lot of time telling us about the progress of "his" brass band. He was very proud that they would be marching in the annual Cape Carnival parade, and that they were all being fitted out in their bright satin outfits for the event. It was wonderful to see how excited Alex was about his new position on the wine farm, because he had struggled financially for years as a professional musician, and he was finally getting the recognition and job security that he so richly deserved.

After a light breakfast on Boxing Day, Alex left for Franschhoek, and we arranged to see him later at the venue. When we arrived there about an hour before the start of the performance we stood at the entrance and scanned the large group of people but we couldn't see Alex anywhere, until we heard a very distinctive explosion of laughter on the other side of the crowd. And that was another standing joke in our family - if we couldn't find Alex in a crowd, all we had to do was listen for the laughter, because that was where he would be.

The venue was in a large and beautiful garden outside a restaurant in Franschhoek, and the evening was warm and mellow. As Alex took to the stage, and he started singing 'C'est si bon', it immediately became apparent that he had a fair-sized group of young regulars who were pretty much his groupies. They were cheering and singing along with him, and, as he always was whenever he was on a stage, he was completely in his element. He was a born performer and he lapped up the appreciative audience, interacting with them in his easy way. As he sang and played his trumpet and accordion with the band, we had a perfect evening under the clear skies and the bright stars, sipping wine and soaking up the music and ambience.

After the performance we left for our flat in Cape Town, leaving Alex behind because he had been offered a bed with one of the band members for the night. I always worried about him when he had to travel late at night after gigs, so I was very relieved to hear that he would be sleeping over. Before saying goodbye to Alex we arranged to meet up a few days later at another wine farm for a wine tasting. William had persuaded Alex to accompany him to a trance party on the 31st of December, so we arranged to meet for the wine tasting, after which William would stay behind with Alex and they would leave for the party the next day. Alex had grumbled to me that he had long since outgrown trance parties, but despite his grumbling he was persuaded to go with his brother. It was clear that Alex was not overly thrilled by the idea of loud trance music assaulting his ears all night, and then trying to get some rest in a tiny tent, but he had always humoured his little brother, so he agreed to go despite not being very keen.

He dropped William off at our flat in Cape Town the morning after the trance party, and we made plans for him to join us for one more dinner on the 3rd of January, because we were due to travel to Knysna for the rest of our holiday on the 4th. Our niece Anne, and her husband and little son joined us for the dinner, and we had a wonderful evening, once again filled with much hilarity and laughter, after which Alex left for his flat in Strand, and our niece and her family left for Stellenbosch.

We left Cape Town the next morning to enjoy the rest of our holiday in our house at Brenton, which is on the opposite side of the Knysna estuary, and we were also planning on travelling to Sedgefield which is very close to Knysna, to visit Derrick, Carly and Owen, because we were going to celebrate Owen's second birthday with them on the 5th of January.

Two days after Owen's birthday, on the morning of 7 January, we woke up to what promised to be another peaceful and relaxing summer day at our holiday home, and we had a leisurely breakfast before driving into town to do some grocery shopping. We had only been back at the house for about an hour when Patrick's mobile phone rang. William and I were sitting on the patio, and Patrick took the call standing a short distance away on the lawn. The call was from my brother, Clive. I didn't hear the conversation, all I heard was Patrick's anguished voice saying, "Alex? How?"

Clive told Patrick that Alex had been killed in a car crash, but he didn't have any more information, except that my ex-husband, Alex's biological father, had phoned to tell him that Alex was dead, and he had asked my brother to let us know.

We were completely pole-axed, and we hugged each other in numb silence. Our entire world had collapsed, and for a few minutes not one of us could say a word as we tried to fathom what had happened. But after a while we had to snap out of it and face a harsh reality – family members needed to be informed, starting with Catherine who was indoors with her friend, and still blissfully unaware of the catastrophe which had struck our family. We also had to inform Derrick that his eldest brother was dead. It is indescribably awful knowing you are about to say something to your child which will shatter their world forever, and the pain of having to do it stays with you forever.

We also had to inform the grandparents, uncles, aunts, and cousins as soon as possible. Alex was a well-known musician in South Africa, as well as further afield, and we knew the accident and his death was likely to be in the local newspapers and on the news, and of course on social media, before long. Every phone call was painful to make because we knew that we were inflicting shock and sorrow on the person we were calling. But it had to be done, over and over, until we felt we had informed everyone who needed to know before the news broke in public. The news had already started spreading, and I received a text message from one of Alex's friends in Sweden: "Is it true about Alex?" she wanted to know. "Yes, it is", I had to reply.

Later that evening, after Catherine's friend had been collected by her mother and taken back home to Port Elizabeth, the four of us sat outside on the patio in the fading light. We just sat there as if we were frozen in time, not speaking, and not moving, and barely able to think. Our world had all but stopped. The sun went down, darkness crept in, it started getting much cooler, but none of us wanted to move. Eventually, Catherine got up and went to her bedroom to be alone, and a while later Patrick went into the kitchen, returning with a platter of biscuits, some sliced cheese and three glasses of wine. We were all operating on autopilot, nothing made sense at all.

Much later that evening Patrick and William eventually went to bed, but I decided to stay outside on the patio by myself. It was past midnight, and I just wanted to be alone, in the silence and solitude, to try and come to terms with what had happened. A few hours later, as the dawn was breaking and it was getting lighter, I saw a grey rabbit silently hop across our dew wet lawn and disappear into the shrubs. It was a new day for that little rabbit, and it was going on with life, as all living creatures do. As I knew I would have to do too, even if I had no desire to.

Just after dawn I quietly crept into bed and dozed off for a while, and when I woke up Patrick showed me the newspaper. On the front page was a news report on Alex's accident and death. It was accompanied by a photo of his badly smashed up car, and we learned from the newspaper report what had happened. A large SUV had broken down on the N1 near Belville, in the middle of the traffic lane, on a bend, and there was no way anyone could have seen the vehicle in the middle of the road until it was too late. Alex was the driver who couldn't see that broken down vehicle in the middle of the road, on a bend, and his life ended when he crashed into the back of the SUV.

How random the Universe is. How terribly random. We had moved our Christmas Day plans from Knysna to Cape Town, because we were worried about Alex driving the four-hour journey between Cape Town and Knysna during the busy Christmas season, and we thought it would be safer for him. Yet, on a sunny Wednesday morning, he died in a car crash on a highway outside Cape Town, on his way to work.

CHAPTER 4

We didn't have much time to dwell on the newspaper report because we needed to get back to Cape Town. The wine farm where Alex had been the music director for less than two years, and where he had been so happy, had offered to hold a private outdoor memorial tribute for his family members, close friends, and the farm staff. On the way to Cape Town we stopped off to see Derrick and Carly, who were not joining us. It would have been very difficult for them to make the journey with two-year-old Owen, so we all agreed that it would be better for them to stay home. Instead, I had offered to post an obituary on their behalf in the local Port Elizabeth newspaper, if they emailed it to me. These were the words they wanted me to share for Alex's obituary:

"We will remember your ability to make a dark day meaningful and comical. Your conviction in confusing times was appreciated, and if you were a farmer you would be reaping good dreams. Rest in Peace".

Our next stop was in Swellendam to see my brother Clive. We had arranged to meet him at a small restaurant on the main road which runs through Swellendam. Alex had often spent time in the small town, and he was very well-known and liked by the locals. He once told us with great amusement that on one of his visits to Swellendam he needed to see the dentist, and after examining his teeth for a while the dentist said to him, "Are you related to Clive?" "Yes! He is my uncle", Alex told the dentist.

According to the dentist Alex looked a lot like Clive and he had the same teeth. That caused much laughter in the family, because it is true that the family resemblance between myself, my brother, two of my four offspring, as well as many of my cousins on my father's side is extremely strong.

As we parked our car in the street, we saw Clive waiting outside the restaurant to meet us. It was one of the worst reunions I have ever had with him, and we just embraced each other in our shared sorrow. There were no words in the world that could express what we felt. Other than myself and Alex's biological father, Clive was the first family member to see Alex after he was born, because he had decided to accompany us to the nursing home. He had waited in the waiting room for the few hours that it took Alex to arrive, and he saw the newborn baby Alex when he was barely an hour old.

When our family entered the restaurant it suddenly became very quiet, as everyone stopped talking, and I saw many people with tears in their eyes, or tears running down their cheeks. Nobody said a word – but it was clear that they knew what had happened.

After a lunch of mostly uneaten sandwiches we resumed our drive to Cape Town, and as we finally approached the city I started to worry about the possibility of seeing news about the accident posted on news posters which usually adorned the lampposts. On the one hand I didn't want to look out for them, and on the other hand I felt compelled to look, but much to my relief there was nothing. It was all over the newspapers and the internet news sites, but at least it was not splashed across any news posters. We had a choice when it came to watching the news or reading the newspapers and internet stories, but the posters would have been very hard to avoid, and I didn't want to be faced with that scenario.

Back in our flat I was almost knocked sideways by the intense pain as I remembered our last Christmas Day with Alex fourteen days earlier, and the last dinner we had enjoyed just a few days before. Everything looked the same, and yet life as I had known it had been lost forever. I looked out of the window where he had parked his little Hyundai, asking us if we thought it was safe to park there. I could still hear his laughter in the room, and I recalled us waving goodbye as he drove away in his little black car.

The owners of the wine farm had arranged a private memorial for family members, very close friends and farm staff on Saturday, 10 January. We had the morning to get through before we left for the farm outside Franschhoek, so Patrick, William, Catherine and I went to the Two Oceans Aquarium to try and occupy our minds, and afterwards we went for lunch at a restaurant on the V & A Waterfront. The Cape Town International Jazz Festival had opened at the V&A Waterfront in Cape Town one day after Alex's accident, and he was on the programme as a performer, but instead of him performing, there was a tribute to him on the opening night. As the co-director said at that event: "He has been part of almost every Jazzathon. We wanted him to be here, but he had to go away".

Yes, he had to go away, no matter how much we also wanted him to be here, and no matter how much we wished he could have stayed. He had to go, but we had to stay.

Sitting in the restaurant, and while we were waiting for the menu, we heard Alex singing, and then playing his trumpet, and we realised they were playing one of his CD's. Where we would once have felt pride and happiness, we now felt pain and defeat. William turned pale with grief and could hardly speak, while the rest of us tried to put a brave face on the situation, as we all struggled through lunch quietly, keeping our thoughts to ourselves.

When we arrived at the wine farm for the memorial later that day, we were completely astounded by the lengths the owners had gone to for the event. Everything was very well organised, from the outdoor seating to the programme of performers in Alex's honour, as well as the catering which they so kindly offered. William was struggling with his emotions even before the event started, and I asked him if he would like to take a short walk with me. I knew he needed to weep in private, so we got up and started walking away rather aimlessly, until one of the owners of the farm asked me if we would like to walk down to the vineyard, and in silent respect he showed us the way. On the walk William sobbed as tears ran down his cheeks unchecked, and we stayed in the vineyard until he had composed himself, before we eventually returned to our seats, where Patrick and Catherine were waiting. The proceedings were opened by the farm brass band which had been founded and directed by Alex. They bravely marched in, dressed in their Cape Carnival outfits which they had so proudly worn just days earlier when they were marching in the parade with Alex, and they played their hearts out, with tears streaming down their cheeks. There were a few speakers, a handful of musicians each did a solo performance, and many memories were shared, as we tried to hold ourselves together throughout the heartrending messages and tributes. Later that evening we were standing outside with a small group of people who had known Alex, when someone told me that a video was playing inside the restaurant which showed a clip of Alex dancing with me at the Oesfees, or Harvest Festival, which had taken place on the farm in March 2008. Alex had played a big role in the decision to hold an annual harvest festival for the workers, and as the music director he had organised many of the bands and musicians. On the day of the festival he had introduced us to several of the farm workers, who clearly adored him, and we had all danced together so joyfully the entire day. Watching that clip would have been too difficult, so we decided to stay outside instead, but I did eventually see the video after someone sent it to me, and it was truly beautiful and heartbreaking at the same time.

 We returned home to Port Elizabeth the day after the private memorial, although Patrick, William, Catherine and I would be returning to Cape Town two weeks later because the owners of the wine farm were planning to hold a large music celebration in Alex's honour, this time for the public.

 Unlike the private memorial, the music celebration was a large event, as we realised when we were given a programme upon our arrival at the gates. Before taking our seats, and before the start of the celebration concert, our small group of close family members had planned to bury Alex's ashes on the farm. He had found true acceptance, happiness, and respect from everyone on the farm, and we were very touched when the owners agreed to let us bury his ashes there. Our small band of family members was led through a beautiful forest, into a clearing next to the river, where a burial place had been prepared for him. After burying his ashes, Patrick and Alex's biological father planted a coral tree, which is now known to the family as Alex's Tree. The moment was still quite unreal, and it was difficult for me to grasp what had happened as I turned away from his resting place, and we returned to take our seats at the concert. It was like being in a different dimension entirely.

We were amazed at the large number of people already seated, and the long queue of people still waiting to get in. Eventually there would be about one and a half thousand people who came together to share in the celebration of Alex's life. Many well-known musicians performed, and there were several speakers, including political figures, councillors, and music personalities who had known and worked or performed with Alex, and once again the tears of the audience and the performers alike flowed freely. We loved Alex as our son, brother, family joker and philosopher, and we would never have imagined that his life and his untimely death would reach that far, bringing politicians, musicians, poets, and speakers together to share their memories and love for him. In many ways we felt like bystanders, watching so many strangers talk about our son, often telling stories about him that we had never heard before.

Several people came up to me to share their stories about Alex and to offer comfort, but as much as they offered me comfort, it was clear that they wanted and needed me to comfort them too. I soon came to understand that as much as they missed and wanted Alex, they found comfort in reaching out to me. Instead of having Alex, they would settle for his mother, and this was especially true of the farm workers and children. They desperately missed Alex, and they saw me, his mother, as a stand-in for him. On the one hand this was quite draining, but on the other hand it did somehow bring me comfort to connect with them at such an emotional time. I could see what he had meant to them, and I tried as best I could to stand in for him, even if I was not the real deal, and they embraced me in every way, as I did them.

CHAPTER 5

After the music celebration we flew back to Port Elizabeth to try and get on with our lives, or what was left of our lives. William stayed with us for a few more days, and then he had to fly back to Johannesburg and get back to his job. It was very hard for me to see him go, because I could see that he was grieving deeply for his brother, but he had always been a very private person, and he didn't share his feelings easily. I wanted to keep him close to us, as any mother would want to, but reality is far more brutal. He had used up his compassionate leave, and he had to return to his job in Johannesburg. It was really difficult to see him check-in, turn back with a wave, and then disappear though the doors. He was clearly heartbroken, and I didn't want him to be alone, and yet I had to let him leave.

Catherine returned to a new year at school, where she chose to keep as low a profile as she could. She stopped inviting friends over, she turned down most invitations to parties or get-togethers, and she preferred to stay at home. Overnight she had turned from a social butterfly enjoying her teenage years, into a reclusive fifteen-year-old. It worried us that our once very sociable daughter had become a loner, refusing any form of social life, and no longer wanting to see her friends after school or on weekends. Until then she had never spent a weekend without one or more friends over to stay, but all that stopped on the day Alex died. Several months later I was talking to William on the phone, and I mentioned our concern about Catherine to him. His reply to me was simple: "Mom, it is not normal to lose a sibling. Just leave her if that is what she wants". We took his advice and hoped that with time she would feel comfortable enough to start socialising with her friends again, but that never happened, and her friends moved on without her. It was a saving grace that she had been very artistic from a young age because she immersed herself in art. We constantly worried about her, but we decided to let her deal with events in her own way, and if she preferred to stay at home, we would have to respect her decision.

The rhythm of life will carry on regardless: Come war, famine, disaster, or tragedy, it is an indisputable reality that life has to go on. Patrick immersed himself in his work and career as an advocate, and I returned to my job as a piano teacher and a class music teacher at the two schools where I worked. We were doing things we had done for many years, and yet our lives had changed so drastically. But the world does keep on turning, life does have to go on, and we have to go on too. There is no alternative.

Patrick found it helpful to keep to his usual routines and activities, and to a large degree I also found it helpful to keep busy with my usual routines and activities, but the reality was that the light had gone out for me. I felt that there was very little joy, nothing to laugh over, and very little happiness to be found in anything. There was so much our family would never experience with him again. His rendition of 'The Laughing Policeman', especially in the car when Patrick was driving and I had to make him stop because we were all laughing so much it was difficult for Patrick to drive, his 'Goon Show' acts, his Oscar Wilde or Noel Coward imitations, his explosive laughter which never failed to get everyone around him laughing too, his hilarious storytelling, his caring personality, and his wonderful talent as a musician. These memories were too painful to think about, let alone talk about.

One evening I was on the computer trying to find a suitable epitaph for Alex and I came across a comment written about him by a music reviewer a few years before he died. For me it said everything about Alex that needed to be said: "Alex is Alex in Wonderland, dancing the streets in his leather winklepickers, caressing the movements of the sea with his accordion. He lives his life with diligence and delight, embroiled in a spontaneous comedy". That is exactly how he did live his life, he was a talented musician and a walking spontaneous comedy, and throughout his short life he seemed to attract only the most positive and joyful people and situations into his ambit. No other words could describe him more accurately.

In the months following his death I received numerous emails from people far and wide, from Sweden, France, Malaysia, Switzerland, South Africa, and further afield. These were mostly from people I had never met, but who had known Alex, some for a longer period of time, and quite a few who told me they had only met Alex once or twice. And yet, they all said the same thing: "We will never forget him, he made us feel so special". I received poems about him, artists sent me paintings of him, and I received many, many emails with stories about him. For me, and for our family, he was just Alex, our beloved son and brother, but to his fellow musicians, friends, and acquaintances, he was many other things. And according to most of them, he was unforgettable. This is something I was told over and over, by everyone who made contact with me.

One of the emails I received was from Jason, who lived on the Isle of Arran. He told me in his email that he had met Alex on Arran in 2003 while Alex was working on the island as a waiter, and that he and his wife had remained in touch with Alex since that time, until his untimely death in 2009. It had taken Jason a few months to get hold of my email address, and it was only after contacting a mutual friend of Alex, who also knew me, that he finally managed to send me the message. I was touched by the fact that he had made such an effort to trace me, and after that, Jason and I kept in touch via emails, just as I did with several other friends of Alex.

In his email Jason included a short poem, which he said was inspired by Alex:

I am a Being Being
born on the trickle of humans humans
from the Cradle of The Rift

Happy being being
I am full to bursting - Boing Being!
At just your spoken gift.

Being human beings
Just *hello* with love - sharing sharing -
and we're aloft!

CHAPTER 6

Back in Johannesburg, William dealt with his grief by becoming more focused on achieving the highest levels he could at work, he enrolled for several more courses, and he also became quite a fitness fanatic, spending his lunch hours at the local gym, working off his energy. He had always been an extremely private person and I didn't want to press him in any way, but he was clearly finding the loss of his brother very hard to deal with. Unfortunately there was not much more I could do other than to try and be there to offer emotional support in whichever small way possible, and hope that with time he would come to terms with his loss.

William decided in early 2010 to move to London. His employers, the CTI Education Group in Johannesburg were very happy to transfer him to their affiliate, the London School of Business and Management in London, and within weeks of his decision to move he had his ancestry visa in his hand, he had a rented room with his friend Seth, he had arranged to let out his house in Johannesburg, and he was on his way to London. Being in London put a spring in his step again, and with him being an ambitious and focused young man, he enjoyed the new challenges at work. He also seemed to love living in London, and it was good to see that he was happy in his new environment. We stopped over in London for a few days in June 2010, after completing the Camino Primitivo from Oviedo to Santiago, and we had a wonderful day together as he showed us his favourite park, Green Park, after which we walked up the Mall. To cap it all, it was Trooping the Colour that day, and we saw the Royal Family on the balcony as they watched the fly over. It was sheer luck, because we had been on the pilgrimage across Asturias and Galicia in Spain for almost three weeks, and we had been out of touch with the news in the UK. We had no idea it was Trooping the Colour that day, so that was quite an exciting surprise.

A few months after that visit Patrick and I discussed the viability of us buying a house in London. We were already travelling to the UK every June because we used to undertake long-distance walks in England as a fundraiser for the Animal Anti-Cruelty League in Port Elizabeth, and it made sense to us that a house in London would give William a place to live, instead of him renting a room, and we could stay in the house whenever we visited London. Also, Catherine had already raised the possibility of studying at a university in London when she finished school, and if she did that she could live in the house with William.

House hunting from a distance can present some real challenges, but these days it is possible to do very detailed searches for properties on the internet, and if there is someone on the other end to physically go and take a look, it is entirely possible to buy a house from afar. After a few likely options, and with William available to go and look at the prospective properties on our behalf, we bought a small three-bedroomed house in Cricklewood, North London, in 2011, and William moved in. Catherine joined him the following year, after she left South Africa for London to start her degree course in English Literature and Creative Writing at Middlesex University.

We were thrilled to have our own base in London and after buying the house we fell into a pattern of travelling to London in June each year, spending a night or two with William and Catherine, and then setting off to do our charity walks, which usually took us between ten days and two weeks, depending which route we were doing and the distance, after which we would spend a few days in London before returning to South Africa. And then we would be back in London for Christmas and New Year. I have always loved London, and I felt very much at home there, as if it was actually my real home, so I was thrilled that we had our own place with our own home comforts. It wasn't a large house, but we were happy with it, especially since it was just off Edgeware Road and close to many shops, pubs and restaurants.

Two-and-a half years after taking up his job at London School of Business and Management William informed us that he had decided to quit his job and strike out on his own as a software developer. He was highly qualified and very experienced, and he felt he needed new challenges. According to William, his new lifestyle of working from home suited him, and he was rapidly building up a large clientele. He was very upbeat about it, but we were less sure about his new way of life as it meant he was spending long hours at his computer, often very late into the night, because he also had clients in other time zones. Whenever we were visiting we noticed that he would sleep until midday, start working in the early afternoon and work until the small hours, only taking the occasional break for meals or free time. We were worried that he never took time off from his work, and we were very concerned that he hardly ever saw the sunlight or got any decent exercise. It was also clear to me that he was still struggling with the loss of his brother Alex, and a certain level of sadness in his demeanour had returned. One day we arrived in London for another of our visits, and I showed him a framed collage of family photos which we wanted to mount on a wall in the house, but he became quite distraught and asked us not to put it up in the house where he would see it. Patrick and I have always filled our home with family photos, and we wanted to put something up in the London house as well, but William told us he couldn't bear the thought of seeing photos of Alex in the house. As he said at the time, "I miss Alex every day and seeing the photos will make it worse". In the end we kept the framed collage of family photos in our bedroom, where we could see them and he didn't have to deal with it, unless he chose to. But it reminded us once again of how he was struggling with his loss, and it worried me that he had chosen his lifestyle of working long hours at home, on his computer, because I knew he was hiding his sorrow from others, and even from himself. We spoke to him about our concerns, but William assured us that he was fine, and he said that down the line he would cut back on his working hours and make more of an effort to get out for exercise. Despite our reservations, we had to accept that it was his life and his choice. After all, he was an adult and he had to make his own decisions. Parenting is so much easier when children are babies, toddlers, and small children, because as parents we can help them deal with their problems and fears, and we can guide them and protect them. But when they are adults we can only offer help and advice, which may or may not be wanted or accepted.

At the end of 2014 Patrick and I were once again going to spend the festive season with William and Catherine in London, but that year we were planning to stay for a while longer because it was Catherine's 21st birthday in late January 2015, and we would be staying in London to celebrate her special day with her. Having a longer time in London gave us the perfect opportunity to make a quick visit to Arran to finally meet with Jason and his wife on the Isle of Arran. We had kept up our correspondence after he sent me the email following Alex's death, and in December I sent him an email asking if they would be home in January because we were hoping to come and meet them. He replied that they would very much like to meet us, so early in January 2015 we booked our train tickets from London to Glasgow and set off to finally meet them in person, on the Isle of Arran. The weather was typical Scottish winter weather, with high winds and stormy seas, but we thoroughly enjoyed the ferry trip across the Firth of Clyde, watching the churning water and the wildness of the wind. It was quite exhilarating. We stayed at a guest house in Brodick for two nights, having arranged with Jason that he would fetch us on the second evening and take us to their house for a visit. It was wonderful meeting people who had known Alex on Arran, and they had many entertaining tales to share about his time there. Alex was renowned for his wacky sense of humour and very caring nature, and we talked late into the night reminiscing about things he had said and done, sharing stories and in so many ways also sharing the joy Alex had always carried around with him and dispensed so freely to everyone around him.

The next morning, before our departure back to London, we took a walk on the beach. The winter weather was in full force, and we didn't go very far, but before turning back, I saw a beautiful pink pebble amongst the other beach pebbles, and I decided to keep it as a memento of our visit, and in memory of where Alex had been in 2003.

We boarded the ferry back to the mainland and then took the train to London, with both of us agreeing that it had been well worth the trip to meet Alex's friends and to see the beautiful island he had told me about in his emails. For as long as we had our house in Cricklewood, that small pink pebble sat on the bookshelf next to my bed, often reminding me of where it came from, and sometimes I would hold it in my hand and think of Alex possibly having walked on that same faraway beach on a small Scottish island.

CHAPTER 7

In 2015 Catherine was in her final year at Middlesex University and she was due to graduate in July, after which she planned to return to South Africa and apply for her ancestry visa. The weeks and months passed quickly, and in June we were on our way to the UK again to do another long-distance walk to raise funds for the Port Elizabeth Animal Anti-Cruelty League. A few weeks earlier Catherine had mentioned to Patrick that she was ill with flu, and I was quite surprised to hear she was ill because she hadn't told me about it, so I started checking on her every day after that to hear how she was doing. At first, she didn't say too much, but after a few days of me checking in on her, she admitted that she didn't seem to be getting any better, instead she seemed to be getting worse. Catherine will not easily admit to being unwell, and with her saying that, I realised it could be serious. It was worrying, but we were due in London in two weeks' time, and the best I could do was to phone her every day to try and keep her spirits up in the meantime. She didn't want to see a doctor, and insisted that she would be okay, although she did tell me during one of our conversations that she had no appetite and couldn't eat much, so I asked William to stock up on ready-made containers of jelly and anything else she wanted to try and eat, until we got there. Meanwhile I phoned her every day to keep in touch, but I was counting the days until we flew to London because I wanted to see for myself what was happening, and to nurse her back to health.

It was a relief when the plane finally touched down at Heathrow Airport and we were very anxious to get to the house. William greeted us at the front door, and behind him we saw Catherine, extremely pale, thin, and obviously quite weak, because she was leaning against the door frame, barely able to stand properly. Despite our long flight and despite us being exhausted, Patrick immediately asked William to phone and make an appointment with a private doctor. "Tell them it is an emergency" he said. Within a few minutes William had managed to get an appointment, and Patrick set off with Catherine on the bus. She could barely walk properly, but she insisted she would manage and didn't want us to fuss too much.

They were away for several hours and to keep myself busy and my mind occupied, I decided to clean the house as I waited anxiously for their return. When they finally got home Patrick told me the doctor had diagnosed pneumonia and she had sent them to a hospital for x-rays, after which they had to return to the doctor's surgery, where the x-rays confirmed her diagnosis. We sent Catherine straight to bed to rest, as we tried to figure out the best way to nurse her back to health. However, we were faced with a dilemma because we were due to start our fund-raising walk the next day, and we didn't want to leave Catherine at a time when she was ill. But cancelling everything would be very difficult, because as usual I had pre-booked and paid for all our accommodation months in advance, and we had received quite a lot of publicity in Port Elizabeth to drum up support for our walk, and thereby raise funds for PE AACL Also, we had a large base of supporters who donated money to the charity when we did the fund-raising walks. Our arrangement was simple: we paid all our own expenses, we did the walks and posted our progress along the way on a Facebook group page set up specifically for that purpose, and donors paid their donations directly into the account of the PE AACL. They desperately need ongoing fund-raising to continue the wonderful work they do with animals in the impoverished townships, and to cancel at that late stage would mean a big loss of financial donations into their charity. After much consideration, we decided to continue with our plans to do the walk, but I promised Catherine I would keep in constant contact with her, she was on a course of medication to treat the pneumonia, and William would be there if she needed him. And if she had an emergency, we would return to London immediately.

As things turned out, I developed a very bad cough the day after we left London, and in all honesty I was relieved not to be in the same house as Catherine. She was ill enough already, and me coughing and spreading germs around the house would make things much worse. I sent her text messages regularly throughout each day to check on her progress, but despite a slight improvement, her follow-up visit to the doctor showed that her one lung was still not healthy, and the doctor prescribed a much stronger antibiotic. The situation made her very despondent, probably because she had been ill for such a long time, and it took quite a lot of encouragement to keep her from getting really downhearted. We finally finished our walk, which had been the full length of the Thames River, from the source near Kemble in the Cotswolds to the Thames estuary beyond London, and when Catherine and William came to meet us at a pub near the Thames Barrier, she seemed to be much better. She was able to walk a decent distance without getting tired, she was no longer very pale, and we were sure that she was on the mend.

We stayed in London for her graduation and then we returned to Port Elizabeth, knowing that Catherine would be following us not long after that. Her student visa would expire soon after graduation, and she would return to South Africa to apply for an ancestry visa, because she was hoping to live and work in London.

Even before Catherine arrived back in South Africa, I had all the required documents ready for her, and the application was expected to be straightforward. One of the requirements for the UK ancestry visa is an x-ray to exclude tuberculosis, and although we knew Catherine had been ill with flu and pneumonia for several weeks, we were sure that she was on the road to recovery. Before leaving London at the end of July she made an appointment with the doctor who was treating her because the doctor had suggested a final check-up before she left the UK, and the doctor then sent Catherine for another set of x-rays to make sure her lung was healthy. The x-rays showed that her affected lung had improved, but it was still not looking as healthy as it should, so the doctor strongly recommended to Catherine that a doctor in South Africa should monitor her situation.

As soon as she arrived in Port Elizabeth I made an appointment with our GP, and after hearing the history of Catherine's flu and pneumonia, she sent her for more x-rays. Since Catherine also needed x-rays for her visa application, I asked our GP if she could have just one set of x-rays done, which we could also use for the visa application after our GP had seen them. That way at least Catherine would not be subjected to unnecessary x-rays, because she had already had three sets taken in London while she was ill. Our GP agreed to this, and I went ahead and made the appointment with the radiologists, explaining that the x-rays were not just for our GP, they would ultimately also be used for a UK visa application, and the receptionist noted this information down with the appointment. She then reminded me that for the purpose of the visa application Catherine needed to bring her passport with her when she came in for the x-rays.

We duly arrived at the radiology department the next day and I waited in the waiting room for Catherine. It worried me that her lung had not healed completely, and I did feel a bit anxious about the results, but I felt relatively positive that everything would be fine. Catherine joined me in the waiting room after the x-rays were done, and we had to wait for about 30 minutes before the report was ready, but when we finally received the radiologist's report it was a huge relief to see that he had noted "no evidence of tuberculosis", which was obviously very important. However, he did mention that her one lung still had a small shadow, which was most likely due to her having been ill with pneumonia. We were not too worried about that because she was going to see our GP the next day, and the GP would monitor it in the coming weeks, so I was confident that all she needed was some good old-fashioned parental 'tender loving care', and she would soon be perfectly well again.

With the final requirement for her application finally ticked off, and with all her documents in order, our proverbial ducks were in a row, and that same evening we did her online application for an ancestry visa, and we booked her appointment at the visa application centre. On the day of her appointment I double-checked and neatly organised all her documents in a file, and we arrived in good time. Catherine went in for her appointment while I waited in the waiting room, fully expecting her to be there for a while as they checked all her documents, but after only ten minutes Catherine emerged from the office with all her documents, together with the visa official, who told me that they no longer accepted TB x-rays done by any hospitals in Port Elizabeth. They only accepted x-ray reports from accredited hospitals in Durban, Pretoria and Cape Town. When I asked him when the regulations had changed, he told me this requirement had been in place for *two years*! To say I was gobsmacked will be putting it mildly. How could the x-ray department in a private hospital in Port Elizabeth not know this? Surely we were not the first people to encounter that problem? After all, we are talking about two years, so they must have been aware of the new regulations. How many unsuspecting visa applicants had wasted their money at that expensive hospital only to be informed that the x-rays were not valid?

This development certainly threw the proverbial spanner in the works for us, but if Catherine wanted the visa, she would have to have her x-rays taken in Cape Town. I kept my fingers crossed as I phoned the radiology department in Cape Town for an appointment, hoping we wouldn't have to wait for several weeks, but I managed to get an appointment in three days' time. The next step was to secure an early morning flight from Port Elizabeth to Cape Town, and a late afternoon flight back to Port Elizabeth after she was finished, on the same day, and fortunately I managed on both counts. After a few frantic hours the crisis was averted and we were back on track, even if it did mean some disruptions and delays. Although this unexpected situation was an inconvenience, our niece Anne kindly agreed to pick Catherine up at Cape Town International Airport, take her to Parow for the x-rays, and get her back to the airport in time for her flight back to Port Elizabeth later in the afternoon.

After dropping Catherine off at the airport early on Thursday morning, I spent the day trying not to conjure up all sorts of negative scenarios, and I was counting the hours until she would phone and tell me she was at the airport, waiting to return home. Despite my niggling concern, I was still expecting Catherine to phone and tell me that the x-rays had been done, all was well, and she was at the airport waiting to get her flight back home. But when she did eventually phone, that was not the case at all. My heart sank when she said the radiologist had told her that they wanted to do a second set of x-rays because they were not satisfied with the first set. Naturally she was worried that this would cause her to miss her flight home, because time would be very tight, but I tried to calm her fears and reassure her we would deal with it if she did miss her flight. I could hear from her voice that she wasn't entirely reassured, but she agreed to phone me as soon as the second set of x-rays had been taken and she had the results. What started off as mildly niggling concerns now became real anxiety. Why did the radiologist want more x-rays? What if it was serious? I wandered around the house and garden aimlessly trying to pass the time, waiting for Catherine to phone me with an update. Finally after about two hours I received a call from her again, but this time she was quite distraught. The second set of x-rays had indicated that her one lung was still not clear, and she had to stay in Cape Town for further tests. This involved sputum tests on three consecutive days, but because it was Thursday and they were closed on a Saturday, she would have to start the tests on the following Monday. Catherine had left Port Elizabeth that morning with her passport, her mobile phone and her wallet with a small amount of money in it. After all, she was only going to be away for one day. And now she was stranded in Cape Town with the clothes on her back, her phone, her passport and hardly any money. But at least she wasn't completely stranded without anywhere to go, because fortunately we had our flat in Greenpoint in Cape Town, and she was still with our niece Anne, who offered to take her to the flat. We always left a key with a friend close by, which meant she could collect the key to get into the flat, so she had somewhere to stay while I tried to figure out what our next step would be. The main thing was for me to get myself to Cape Town, so I immediately started looking at flights for the next morning. Catherine would not only need clothes and money, I thought some parental moral support would also probably be quite welcome. It was panic stations until I finally managed to secure a seat on an early morning flight to Cape Town for the next day, and later that afternoon my stress was somewhat relieved when Catherine sent me a message to let me know that she was safely in the flat and that her money had stretched far enough for her to buy something to eat and drink for the night. She had bought a pizza, a bottle of wine and a packet of rusks, which are a South African speciality, similar to Italian biscotti, but usually enjoyed with a mug of tea of coffee. She was safe, she had food and drink, and I knew she would be fine until I got there.

After Patrick and I had finished supper that evening I sent William a Skype message with the latest news, and although he was sorry about all the trouble we had to go through, he said he was sure that the test results would be fine, and he reassured me that he didn't think there was anything to worry about. I wanted to agree with him, but there was a small and persistent voice in my head that did make me worry. It was a trying time for all of us, most of all for Catherine.

Early the next morning I was on my flight to Cape Town, and Catherine and I spent a very pleasant weekend taking advantage of our unexpected "holiday" in Cape Town. Greenpoint is a vibrant place to be, and it is just a short walk away from the Sea Point Promenade, which is a very popular place for taking long walks along the sea front of the Atlantic Ocean. Going in the other direction from our flat, it is a short walk to the V&A Waterfront, with the many restaurants and tourist attractions. So all in all, things could have been a lot worse for us than having to spend a few days in Cape Town, and we made the most of it.

On the following Monday morning we were up very early and ready to start the trip to the medical centre in Parow for the first of the three sputum tests. It took us almost an hour by Uber to the medical centre every morning, and because we had to be there at eight o'clock every morning, it meant we were in peak traffic each time. For three consecutive days we made the long trip there and back again, using our time in the Uber to make plans for an interesting day to keep us occupied. There was plenty to do, but we preferred to do things which were walking distance from the flat because we didn't have a car, so we took walks through the city centre to Cape Town Gardens, we walked along the Sea Point Promenade, and each afternoon we lifted our spirits by treating ourselves to lunch in a different restaurant, usually accompanied by one of the many craft beers on offer.

Finally, the last sputum test was done, and we could return to Port Elizabeth. The results would take a full 8 weeks, so it was going to be a long and anxious wait for us. Just before Catherine left the medical centre, the nurse who had carried out the sputum tests earnestly told Catherine to "trust in the Lord, and your test results will be fine". We both managed to keep a straight face until we were outside, and then we both had a good giggle and shook our heads in disbelief. If only life could be that simple! Still, we both agreed that she had meant it kindly.

About two weeks after we had returned from Cape Town Patrick saw our GP in a shopping queue where they struck up a conversation, and when Patrick mentioned what had transpired, she told him that there was a TB test which gave results within 48 hours. It would not suffice for the visa application, but we felt it was worth having the test done, if only to reassure ourselves that Catherine did not have TB. If we knew she was fine, it would make the long wait for the officially accredited tests from Cape Town less stressful. We were certain it was just one of those unfortunate inconveniences, and the TB results would show that everything was fine. Right? Not at all. Very, very wrong. The 48-hour TB test was positive. And we were all absolutely floored.

Catherine didn't appear to be ill any longer, she wasn't coughing and she was very fit. But the test was very clear – it showed a positive result for TB. Our GP referred Catherine to a pulmonologist, and after an examination and careful scans of her lungs he agreed that she seemed to be the least likely patient to have TB. She had absolutely no symptoms at all, except for a very small mark on her lung, and he told us that occasionally the 48-hour tests can show a false positive result. He admitted that it did not happen often, but it had been known to occur. That was a small glimmer of light, although I suppose it was more a case of grasping at straws, but we still tried to be cautiously optimistic as we anxiously waited for the tests from Cape Town.

After eight long and anxious weeks, Catherine and I were back in the consulting rooms of the pulmonologist for the results, and the news was devastating. Catherine did have TB after all. That meant all her plans had to be shelved until she had completed her treatment, which would take at least six months. The diagnosis of TB brings so many thoughts and fears to mind. We were faced with the potential risks to others who had been with Catherine, including ourselves and William, our niece Anne who had picked her up at the airport, taken her to lunch and then, after the unfortunate x-ray result, taken her to our flat. Our niece has lupus, and I was very worried about the risk to her, so I phoned her with the news and suggested she contact her doctor and discuss the potential risks. And I was very worried about my stepmother Colleen, who is very fond of Catherine and took her out to lunch almost every week while she was in Port Elizabeth. Colleen had been ill with bronchitis during the winter, and I was concerned that she may have been at risk of infection with TB, so I asked her to contact her doctor and get his advice on it. But where did we draw the line when informing people? I had asked the pulmonologist at the last consultation when he gave us the results what we should do regarding those who had been in contact with Catherine in the past two months, and he wasn't particularly worried about that. He told us that the vast majority of South Africans are exposed to TB at some time or other, but those with a healthy immune system can resist developing TB. It was mainly in cases of serious illnesses, such as flu, malaria or HIV, that latent TB could be triggered into active TB. In his words: "We have all been exposed anyway, so just inform those you think are at risk, and don't worry too much about it". Naturally we were very upset by the diagnosis, but we were grateful that at least it was treatable, and the pulmonologist was very optimistic about the road ahead, which did help to reassure us in a way.

After he had given us the results and discussed the details of what we would have to do, I asked him if he was prepared to prescribe the medication for Catherine so that she could get it at a pharmacy and not at the state clinic. I knew that most TB patients in South Africa had to rely on the state TB clinics, and I pitied the poor souls who had no choice other than to sit in crowded waiting rooms once a week for most of the day, to collect their medication. It was, and still is, a very sad situation. Old people, infants, and the poverty stricken who are weakened from a lack of food all suffer the worst side-effects of the TB medication due to weakness and debility. And many of those at the TB clinic also have HIV/Aids at the same time as they have TB, yet despite their suffering, they are expected to sit for hours in a crowded, stuffy room and wait for attention, which is often very cold and uncaring. Many TB patients give up and stop going to the clinics for their medication because they are so weakened, and the treatment makes them feel so terribly ill. In many cases this has resulted in the development of drug resistant tuberculosis, which is a far more dangerous form of TB, and is very difficult to treat successfully.

Fortunately the pulmonologist told me that he had no problem giving us a prescription to cover the full twenty-four weeks, but he warned me that our only difficulty may be getting the drugs, because the state clinics had preference when it came to the supplies, which is completely understandable. Once again, we were very fortunate. Patrick phoned his brother Earl, who is a pharmacist, and Earl assured him that he would be able to get the full six-month supply of drugs for Catherine.

The first batch was delivered the following day, to be followed a few days later by the rest of the supply, and she had to clear out an entire shelf of her wardrobe to make space for the many boxes of drugs. But we were extremely happy to have her medication stocked up for the next six months, and it is in situations like these that one can see things in perspective. We had so much to be grateful for. We could afford to see a pulmonologist who was prepared to prescribe the drugs for us, and we had a family member who could source the drugs for us. Many people are not as fortunate, and we were well aware of that.

The treatment for TB involves several strong drugs, every day, for a full twenty-four weeks, and the drugs are very potent with extremely unpleasant side-effects. But knowledge helps us take more informed decisions, and both Catherine and I spent a lot of time researching the side-effects and how to counter them. The information we found on the internet looked rather grim to say the least, but right from the start Catherine decided that she would be in control of her illness and the treatment, and she did as much reading about it as she could. Taking control of her treatment gave her the strength, emotionally and physically, to face the next six months head-on, which she did with great determination and with no complaints.

Once we had all come to terms with Catherine's diagnosis we revisited the question of how the Cape Town radiologist had immediately detected a potential problem with Catherine's lung, and yet the Port Elizabeth radiologist not only completely missed a very serious disease, he even specifically stated on Catherine's x-ray report that there was no evidence of TB. It says in black and white: "no evidence of tuberculosis", and it is signed by the radiologist. And then there was the question of why that particular radiology department was still doing x-rays for visa applications when they were no longer accredited, and had not been for two years. This happened at a very well-known, and extremely expensive, private hospital in Port Elizabeth. It is no surprise that the UK visa office no longer accepted TB clearance x-rays from any radiology departments other than specifically accredited radiologists.

CHAPTER 8

The human mind is quite remarkable in finding something positive in the most difficult times. After the initial shock of Catherine's diagnosis, we found ourselves saying: 'Well at least she only has "normal" TB and not the drug resistant strain, because the drug resistant strain is much more dangerous and difficult to treat'. I never thought we would see "normal" TB as something to be grateful for, but knowing how dire the drug resistant strains are, the good old "normal" strain was easier to come to terms with. And then of course, we were able to see a good pulmonologist as well as buy the drugs up front. We knew we were very fortunate, and we had a lot to be thankful for.

There is more than enough good information available online on how to counter, or even prevent, serious side-effects when taking the strong TB drugs, and right from the start of her treatment Catherine started taking the best pro-biotics available, as well as a few highly recommended supplements to deal with some of the worst side-effects. She has a very strong will, and to deal with her illness she made sure she knew what to do to stay as healthy as possible, physically and emotionally. This positive attitude paid off, because other than losing quite a lot of her beautiful long hair, and developing a mild rash, Catherine had no serious side-effects at all. And never for one moment did she show that she was despondent about what had happened.

Naturally, it was a big disappointment for all of us that she would have to delay her plans to return to London, but we could still look forward to spending Christmas and New Year with William in London. Catherine would have to apply for a holiday visa, but at least that does not require TB clearance, and because of the cost involved in getting her a holiday visa, we agreed that she did not need to return to South Africa with us in the New Year. Instead, she could spend more time in London with her brother. Of course, that meant she had to take enough TB medication with her to cover her for almost two months, and her suitcase would be pretty much filled with tablets. I could just imagine the suspicion all those boxes of tablets in one suitcase would cause, and there was no doubt in my mind that her luggage would be opened and checked by border control at the airport.

After the previous few stressful months it was wonderful to be in London for our Christmas holiday. We all enjoyed the hustle and bustle of London, the pubs, the shops, and the general atmosphere as Christmas drew near, and it was good to see William again. On New Year's Eve Patrick and I took William and Catherine to an Ethiopian restaurant in Cricklewood to see in the arrival of 2016, and a few days later we returned to South Africa, leaving a very happy daughter in London for a few weeks. She was thrilled to be back in her own little bedroom in the London house, and she was happy to be with her brother William again, even if it was only for a few weeks.

CHAPTER 9

Back from London, we were soon immersed in our usual routines of work and the general humdrum of life. As we usually did after our holidays, we travelled to Sedgefield to visit Derrick, Carly and Owen, and we also started preparing for the Knysna Celtic Festival with the pipe band, where we would be playing in the piping competition at the end of February.

Catherine finally arrived back in Port Elizabeth on 19 February to see out the rest of her 'enforced' stay with us, and I contacted William later that day via Skype to let him know that she had arrived safely. After a brief chat about everyday things I said goodbye to him, agreeing to chat again soon. And then life just jogged along as usual.

One week after Catherine arrived back from London Patrick and I were preparing to travel to Knysna for the Knysna Celtic Festival for the piping competition. We were due to play in the competition on Saturday, and then Patrick and I would have an early lunch with Derrick, Carly and Owen on Sunday, before returning home to Port Elizabeth. Catherine would stay at home to hold the fort, as she was taking care of all our pets, although our usual house-sitter would stay in the house for safety and security reasons. Late on Friday night before our departure, just before bedtime, I sent William a short Skype message to let him know that we would be out of town for the weekend, and I told him I would be in touch when we got back. We didn't chat every day, or even every week, because he was usually quite busy, but I usually did let him know when we were going to be out of town, in case he needed to contact us.

After many long hours of hard work, and a great deal of marching up and down a sports field with the pipe band, we all set off for Knysna looking forward to a happy weekend. Our fellow band members were a fun-loving group, who enjoyed a good time, and we had all booked into the same holiday park, where we would be sharing chalets. I had told Derrick and Carly about the massed band parade on the Saturday morning, and together with Owen, they were among the crowds who were lining the main street of Knysna to watch the bands go past. When I asked Owen afterwards what he thought of the bagpipes he replied, "They were very, very loud". He seemed more impressed by our kilts and band outfits, and he was especially interested in our sgian dubhs, a type of dagger, which we kept tucked in our socks. We didn't have much time to chat because our pipe band was due to play in the competition, so Derrick, Carly and Owen left for Sedgefield, and we arranged to see them at their house for lunch the next day.

After a fun-filled weekend, we arrived back home on Sunday evening, ready for a new week. Monday was a rather busy day, and it was only on Tuesday morning that I realised I had forgotten to let William know we were back. I sent him a quick Skype message just to let him know we were home, thinking we could catch up with a chat another time. When he didn't reply, I sent another message in case he had missed the first one, and I was rather surprised that he didn't respond to that either, because he always responded very quickly to messages or phone calls. Whenever we phoned him and he missed the call, he would call back within minutes. It was very unlike him to not respond. But I reckoned he probably had other things to do besides sit at the computer on Skype all the time, so I decided to try again the next day in case he was out and about. I was sure that by then he would probably have seen my messages and would have replied. But on Wednesday morning there was still no reply to my previous messages on Skype. This was so out of character that I wondered if he had gone to visit a friend out of town, and I decided to call him on his mobile phone, but his phone was on voicemail. William had never been completely out of touch for long, and I wasn't sure what to make of it, so I mentioned to Catherine that I had been trying to contact him but he was not replying. Catherine reassured me that sometimes William took a few days off from his work, carried his bedding down into the lounge, and spent some time just resting on the sofa watching sport, usually cricket, until he had recharged his batteries. This sounded like a perfectly reasonable explanation to me. It made sense that he wasn't reacting to Skype messages or phone calls if he was taking time off from his computer, and maybe also his mobile phone.

William had his own software developing company and he was still working from home, something both Patrick and I were not particularly happy about. We had been very concerned about his lifestyle for quite some time already, and when we were visiting him in London for Christmas in 2015, we noticed that he also seemed to be more anxious and had difficulty relaxing and getting a decent night's sleep. The day before Patrick and I left London after our Christmas holiday I went into William's bedroom where he was working on his computer, and I sat down on his bed to have a chat with him about our concerns. I told him we were worried that he worked such long hours and that he hardly ever went outdoors, but he assured me that he was planning to get more exercise as soon as the weather improved, and he also told me he was thinking about getting himself a little dog because he missed our dog Shadow, who lived with us in South Africa. He said he would like to get a dog similar to "my Shaddie" as he called Shadow, and he told me he was planning to take his dog for walks and runs every day in Gladstone Park. But he was waiting for Spring, when it would be warmer. Shadow saw William as her most beloved human, and whenever he visited us she would be the happiest dog on the planet, leaping around with joy. She would stay by his side day and night, even sleeping on his bed. But then when he left again, she would pine for several days, and look at us with her mournful face, as if to say, 'Where has my William gone?' It always took a few days before she came to terms with his departure, and during that time we would have to spend a lot of time consoling her.

Despite our worries about his lifestyle, I did feel a lot less concerned when William said he was planning to get a dog and take it out to the park for walks and runs, but my parting words after that conversation will always stay with me. As I stood up and turned to leave his room, I said to him, "We do worry about you William, you work too hard. We have already lost one son, and we will never survive losing another son".

And his reply was, "I know Mom. Don't worry, I promise you I will be fine".

Even after Catherine's explanation, I continued to send a few text messages, just in case William picked up his phone and saw them. At that stage I hadn't mentioned it to Patrick because I thought, and hoped, that Catherine was right and that he was just having some time away from his computer and his phone. But by Thursday morning I was feeling less sure about it, and I decided that it would be worth trying to call him on the landline, even if he was resting and even if it meant I would disturb him, because he hadn't responded to any Skype messages, mobile phone calls or text messages since Tuesday morning. There was no reply on the landline either, and that is when I started to feel the first stabs of panic, so I decided to call his friend Seth and ask him when he had last spoken to William.

The reply I got from Seth was very alarming - he told me that he had been trying to contact William since the previous week, and he couldn't understand why he wasn't responding to any messages or calls. Initially I tried to convince myself that there must be a reasonable explanation, but when I told Catherine what Seth had said, I could see that she didn't agree with me. She was clearly upset, and as much as I tried to reassure her that there was no point in jumping to any conclusions until we knew more, she dismissed my words.

"Something bad has happened. I just know it", she insisted.

My mind refused to accept that possibility. I quite simply couldn't believe that there was anything other than a perfectly good explanation why William hadn't responded to messages and phone calls. But darker thoughts were forcing themselves into my consciousness, despite my denial.

Patrick didn't know that I had been trying to contact William for a few days because until then I was so sure he would eventually reply to my messages that I hadn't mentioned it. But what Seth told me changed everything. There was no denying the reality any longer that William hadn't been responding to any messages or phone calls for quite some time. When Patrick arrived home from work, I finally told him that I hadn't been able to contact William for two days, and that Seth had been trying to make contact since the previous week, without any success.

For the rest of that evening we were plunged into a complete nightmare scenario. The only person we could ask to go and see if he was okay was his friend Seth, so we reluctantly asked him if he would go around to our house and see if William was there. He agreed to go after work and let us know, and we spent the next few hours almost paralysed with fear and worry, waiting for Seth to call. When he finally called, he told me that he was outside the house, the lights were on, the lounge curtains were drawn, there were dishes in the kitchen sink, but despite persistent knocking and calling through the letterbox there was no response. There was no other option, I had to ask him to phone a locksmith to remove the lock.

Denial of reality is a very powerful emotion, and despite everything pointing to a terrible outcome, I was still in denial. Surely it was possible that he may have popped out to the corner shop? Or perhaps he had gone away for a few days and lost his phone? My mind was not prepared to contemplate the worst. Which parent will believe the worst until they are faced with it? We always try and see a small light of hope.

If we had known what Seth would find, we would not have asked him to go into the house. I don't know what else we could have done, but I do know we wouldn't have wanted his best friend to find him. William had indeed taken his bedding into the lounge, and he was lying on the sofa. But he was dead. And had been dead for several days.

Patrick and Catherine were next to me in the study when I took the call from Seth. He told me he was in the lounge, and William was on the sofa, but he wasn't moving.

"Is he not moving at all Seth?" I asked.

He replied, "No".

And then I asked, "Is he breathing?"

Again Seth replied, "No".

In pointless desperation I asked, "Are you sure?"

And he replied "Yes, I am sure".

From somewhere far away I heard myself saying, "Will you please call the police Seth?"

There was no need for me to tell Patrick and Catherine. They knew. Lightning had struck twice in the same place. We had lost another son. We didn't know what had happened or why, and we didn't even know when. All we knew was that William was dead.

CHAPTER 10

As the three of us tried to remain standing amidst a world which was falling apart around us, we could hear the neighbours and their friends next door laughing and partying. They were having a raucous house-warming party. While one family was experiencing utter heartbreak and devastation, another family was enjoying a wonderful party.

Light and Darkness. Joy and Sorrow. Sunshine and Shadow. The two sides of life that happen every day across the world.

When the police arrived at the house in Cricklewood, an officer spoke to me briefly to explain that William had passed away, and that they were removing his body. He told me that the coroner would contact me the next day and would keep in contact to let us know what had happened. After speaking to the police, and before I could ring off, Catherine urgently told me to speak to Seth again, and ask him to please check on her budgie, Jo. She had left Jo in the care of William, and she suddenly realised that Jo may not have been fed or watered for a few days. Seth checked on the little budgie, and amidst our shock and sorrow, we could at least be grateful for the news that Jo was still fine. Seth fed him and gave him water, but we still had to think about what we would do about him.

The three of us were completely crushed, and incapable of grasping what had happened. If Alex's death had been an earthquake that brought everything tumbling down around us, William's death was a tsunami that swept what remained completely away.

We decided it was too late to phone any family members, and nothing would change between then and the next morning, so we kept the news to ourselves overnight. After a very miserable and sleepless night, my first call was to Derrick, when, once again, I had to deliver the terrible news that his brother was dead. He had grown up as the middle son, with two brothers, and now he was the only son left. For a parent it is a soul-destroying call to make, and I will never forget the awfulness of knowing I was about to deliver such devastating news, for the second time.

That was only the first call, as Patrick and I spent the entire morning phoning close family members and a select few friends to break the terrible news. It was only when we thought we had informed everyone necessary that we posted the news on social media for William's friends, although by then the news had started to seep out via some of his friends in London.

Later that day I received a call from the coroner's office in London who patiently talked me through what needed to be done. She said there would be no need for a family member to make a formal identification because Seth had already identified William to the police when he found him. And then came a bombshell. She told me that they had found heroin paraphernalia in the house.

"Did you know your son was using heroin?" she asked me.

It felt like an electric shock to my system. No, I hadn't known. None of us had known. And we had been there just a short while before, for a full month. Despite being worried about William's lifestyle of all work and no play, and with hindsight, despite noticing that he had lost weight and seemed unwell, we had never suspected that he was using heroin. It was only later when I was speaking to Seth that he told me he had visited William on 14 February, and he had found out about William using heroin when he was there. Seth said he had been very upset about it, and he had warned William that if he did not promise to quit, he would tell me what was happening. But William had promised Seth that he was going to quit, and insisted he was going to do it on his own, without any medical help. He said he was waiting for Catherine to leave, and she was due to leave for South Africa on 18 February. He didn't want her to be there when he was going through the withdrawal process. That sounded very typical of him. William had always been a very private and independent person, and he would have tried to deal with his addiction on his own instead of getting medical help. Despite the high risks involved, he would have tried to quit by going 'cold turkey'.

According to the autopsy, William died of 'morphine toxicity'. There was no evidence of foul play, and it was not suicide. What had he taken? Why had he taken it? What had happened? When had he died? Why had he died? Had things gone wrong during the withdrawal process? We don't know. And we will never know. All we do know is that the last time Catherine and I spoke to him was on 19 February. And he was found on 3 March. We will never know more than that.

Since a very young age William had been a very motivated, ambitious, and hard-working young man. He would set his goals high, and he would always achieve them within his set timeframe. Although he seemed happy, we knew that he had never recovered from the death of his brother Alex. They had been extremely close, and he was heartbroken when Alex died. Did he finally turn to drugs to ease his pain? Yes, I believe that is very likely. Does it torment me that I didn't understand the depth of his pain? Yes, it does, every day. But I have also learned to accept that no matter how well we think we know and understand our children, we quite simply do not know everything about them. Our family had always discussed the risks of drugs very openly and without judgment, and yet there came a time in his life where he felt the need to dull his pain with heroin. That is a heavy burden for me to carry, and I will always question why I didn't see what was happening. And how I missed the possible warning signs.

CHAPTER 11

On the advice of the coroner, I did not attend the inquest. She told me I was free to do so, but she would not recommend it because the details of an autopsy at an inquest are by their very nature deeply distressing. I took her advice, because knowing any more distressing details would not help us in any way. Nothing would bring William back, and there was no point in tormenting myself or our family any further by attending the inquest. Patrick and I had decided that I would fly to London to deal with William's affairs because we had just returned from a month-long holiday in London, and he needed to be back at work. Although I had several piano pupils, it was easy enough to cancel the lessons for as long as it would take me to deal with everything in London.

However, my journey back to our house in Cricklewood would have to be postponed until the police had given me clearance to enter the house. In the meantime, I had to wait at home in Port Elizabeth, trying to come to terms with what I would have to do when I got to London. There would be the unenviable trip to our house where I would have to face the living room and sofa where William spent his last hours, and I would have to go through his private things in his bedroom to find personal documents and everything else that is required by officialdom after someone has died. Looking through someone else's private drawers and personal belongings or opening mail addressed to another person, even close family, goes completely against my grain. But in this instance, I had no choice, and it was going to be very, very hard to do.

After finally getting the all-clear from the police, I booked my flight to London, and a few days later Patrick and I bade each other a heavy-hearted farewell, as he returned home to Catherine, and I made my way to the boarding gate to await the departure of my plane to Johannesburg, where I would have to spend a few hours before my later flight to London. Thank goodness airport toilets are always bustling with passengers who are coming or going their own way, with little time to pay attention to any fellow travellers, because I spent a great deal of my time in the toilets, where I could close a door, flush the toilet, and weep silently into my tissues. After boarding the plane, I was very relieved to see that the flight to London was not fully booked, and I was the only passenger in my row of seats. I didn't feel like talking to anyone, because any polite conversation was bound to include questions about my trip to London, and I didn't want to talk to anyone about that or anything else. All I wanted was to get to London without any problems.

Upon my arrival at Heathrow airport I joined the long queue of tired passengers at passport control and inched my way forward slowly, just trying to remain focused on getting through things one minute at a time. Finally, it was my turn and I handed my passport to the immigration officer.

"Are you here on holiday", he asked me.

"No, our son passed away. I am here to arrange his cremation", I replied, trying not to burst into tears.

The officer, who had started off very much as an official, instantly changed his demeanor, as he silently and quickly stamped my passport without asking any more questions, softly telling me he was very sorry and wishing me well. That was my first hurdle cleared and I was through customs, but the next hurdle was less easy. It took me a long time to connect with an Uber driver because reception in the Heathrow terminal was very unreliable and I kept losing the connection. After what felt like an eternity, I finally managed to connect to a driver named Mohamed, and I was very relieved to hear that he was on his way. However, that relief didn't last long, because within a few minutes he called me back and told me his car had broken down. So, I had to start the whole process again, and after about thirty minutes I finally managed to book another Uber driver, also named Mohamed. And he turned out to be a real gem of a man. My first stop was to be at the Wembley Police Station to collect the house keys, and I didn't know how I would manage to get from there to our house in Cricklewood because I wouldn't have WiFi or data on my phone to contact an Uber driver again, and I was absolutely too shattered to figure out which bus to take.

On the trip from the airport Mohamed asked me why I was in London, and I told him that my son had died, and I needed to arrange his cremation and deal with his affairs. I am sure that was the last reply he was expecting, and he looked quite shocked, but he was very polite and asked a few more questions, so I thought I may as well ask him if he could wait for me while I went into the Police Station to collect the house keys. He immediately agreed and said he would wait for as long as I needed him. And it turned out to be quite a wait, because I was at the Police Station for more than twenty minutes. But Mohamed patiently waited for me all that time. I knew I would be billed for it, but that was the least of my problems. He was very kind and thoughtful at a time when I needed it very much, and he truly was an angel in my time of need.

When I finally arrived at the house, William's bedding was still on the sofa and some used plates and glasses were still on our small dining room table in the living area. Everything looked the way it would have looked if he was upstairs in his bedroom, working at his computer. Only one thing was out of place. The glass coffee table which always stood in the middle of the lounge floor had been moved aside for the police to remove his body. I didn't even bother to take my suitcase upstairs to our bedroom, I just deposited it right where I was standing, gathered his bedding from the sofa and put everything into the washing machine, and then

I took the dirty dishes to the kitchen and washed them. After that I moved the glass table back into place and wiped it clean. All I wanted to do was to remove anything which would remind me of his last moments.

Despite being exhausted, there was no time to rest. I had made an appointment to meet the funeral director at the funeral home later that day to make the arrangements for William's cremation. William's friends Bart and Tracey lived in London, and Tracey worked in a funeral home. Even before I left for London she had contacted me and offered to help me in any way she could. Tracey and Bart themselves had suffered a tragedy when their infant son Kristian died tragically as a newborn a few months earlier, and I recalled how deeply upset William had been by their tragedy. She had arranged to meet me at the funeral home and assist me with everything as far as she could. Sometimes in our darkest hours, angels on earth come our way, and, like Mohamed, Tracey was another angel who was there for me when I needed help, taking care of so many official details and doing whatever she could to make things a bit easier for me.

She had sent me the directions to the funeral home, with instructions on which trains to get and where to change over, because it was quite a journey, including several changes along the way. With the directions in my pocket, I set off at a fast pace through Gladstone Park to the Dollis Hill Tube Station, but I was halfway through the park when I remembered that I hadn't taken any clothes for William. He needed to be properly dressed for his cremation after all. Time was tight, but I turned around and hurried back to the house to find some clothes, intending to take something smart because William had always been very particular about what he wore, and he always had very good taste in clothes. Back in his room I rummaged through his wardrobe and drawers, looking for a good shirt and suit, which I knew he had. But I could only find t-shirts, jeans and board shorts, and his jeans needed a wash so they wouldn't do. In somewhat of a panic I looked in all the drawers and the wardrobe once again, but I couldn't find anything smart at all. Eventually I had to settle on the nicest T-shirt and board shorts I could find, and I also grabbed a pair of clean underpants, as if that mattered.

The journey to the funeral home took a long time, and after what felt like an eternity, I finally arrived to find Tracey waiting at the door. Her warm embrace meant a great deal to me at a time when I was having to deal with something no parent ever wants to think about, but she understood, because she had experienced the same terrible loss of a child. She stayed with me as the funeral director went through all the details, asking me many questions about what I wanted them to do. Patrick and I had decided we wanted the cremation to be as simple as possible, with his friends saying a few words if they wanted to, and with them playing his favourite music. Nothing elaborate, just intimate and simple.

When the funeral director asked me if I had brought clothes to dress William in, I told her that I had only been able to find casual wear despite looking everywhere for his smart clothes, and that William would have to enter the Pearly Gates dressed casually, in a T-shirt and board shorts. Despite the sad and sombre situation, we all had a little laugh at the thought.

Later that evening, after I had returned home, I was in William's bedroom, starting on the hard task of sorting through his things when there was a knock on the door. It was Seth. He had two shopping bags filled with easy to prepare meals, a bottle of milk and a carton of fruit juice.

"I thought buying food would be the last thing on your mind, so I brought you something", he told me, as he handed me the bags.

Seth was another angel on this earth, who was there for me during that terrible time, and we spoke until late in the evening about what had happened. It worried me that Seth had found his friend William the way he had, and it was clear that the experience had been deeply traumatic for him. William and Seth had met on their first day of high school as young thirteen-year-old boys, and they had remained close friends. Some may say 'partners in crime', as they often got up to mischief together, and their friendship had lasted since those high school days into adulthood. Seth offered to help me deal with all William's accounts and his work clients as far as he could, which was a huge relief because I didn't know where to start. The mountain we had to climb was going to be very high and very tough, but Seth said he would help me as much as possible, and he was true to his word.

The next morning, while I was sorting and tidying William's things, I found all his suits and beautiful shirts packed away in a suitcase, the one place I had not looked before hurrying off to the funeral home. It made me feel really sad to know I hadn't found them in time, but I couldn't dwell on it because I had to get started on the difficult task of tidying his room, clearing out things he would no longer need, and packing all his personal belongings away in boxes. It was a long and soul-destroying time, as I went through his drawers, gathering his documents and sorting through several years of paperwork that he had accumulated as a software developer. I was sure if someone could read the strange symbols of "computer language", they would find it useful, but my only mission was to get all his documents together, sort out his personal things, keep what we needed to keep, and throw away what we wouldn't need or want. I simply did not have the energy to try and figure out what to do with all his software developer's notes and papers, and I put everything into the recycling bin, which was soon close to overflowing. After the very long and emotionally draining first day, I sank down onto the sofa and when I turned the TV on, it was on Sky Sport, on the cricket channel. Just as Catherine had said, "William will chill in the lounge on the sofa, and watch cricket".

There was an endless list of things to do, but the most important thing I needed to do was to open a bank account and transfer all the utility bills into my own name. William had always dealt with the utility bills, and soon his bank account would be frozen, which meant the bills would not be honoured. Fortunately, he had been meticulous in keeping all his official paperwork and documents neatly together, so I had all the accounts and account numbers. But first, I needed a bank account. Early the next morning I took a bus to the bank in Golders Green, and within minutes I was approached by an assistant asking me if she could help me. I told her that I needed to open a bank account. "Do you have an appointment?" she asked me, in a rather clipped voice. When I replied that I didn't, she told me I would have to make an appointment, and she took me across the floor to the appointment book. Unfortunately, the next appointment available was a whole week away, on the very day I was due to leave London. I explained my predicament to her and told her that I had to open an account before I left otherwise none of our bills would be paid. Although she was not very happy about fitting me in before her next customer, she was gracious enough about it and agreed to help me. She could clearly see that I was at the end of my tether, and it was a very urgent situation, but she was in a hurry to deal with me as quickly as possible, and it was a very difficult time for me to be thinking of all the details she wanted to know. My foggy brain was struggling to come up with things such as passwords for internet banking and all kinds of other information she was demanding from me. How does a person manage to answer all the tricky questions required to open a bank account, not to mention think of a suitable banking password, when your mind is shattered? She was clearly trying to do her job, but she was also under pressure to do it fast because her next customer was due.

Things were going reasonably well until she told me that I needed an original utility bill from South Africa to show proof of my address there. Not a copy, an original bill, nothing else would do. I had no idea how I would manage to achieve that because I only had a few more days left in London, but I promised to provide it as soon as possible, one way or the other. As soon as I was back at the house I phoned Patrick, who said he would courier the document to me immediately, and two days later, with the original utility bill showing proof of my address in Port Elizabeth in hand, I was back at the bank. Thank goodness everything went smoothly, and at last I had a bank account. A small but important victory.

Over the next few days Seth came around after work every evening and spent as much time as he could, helping me transfer utility bills into my name, cancelling subscriptions in William's name, including his mobile phone subscription. The list was quite long, but every evening he spent many hours with me, just patiently working his way through each item. Nothing seemed too much trouble for him, and I will forever owe him a huge debt of gratitude for what he did for me.

CHAPTER 12

After a harrowing time in London I finally boarded the plane back to Cape Town. Patrick and Catherine were already in Cape Town for a short holiday, and I was going to join them there. They had been to the annual Solms Delta Oesfees, or Harvest Festival, on the wine farm in Franschhoek, where Alex used to work, and where he was buried. At the very first Oesfees Alex was so proud and excited to see what he had helped put together for the local musicians, especially the farm workers.

"Will you come again?" he asked us more than once on that wonderful day.

"We wouldn't miss it for anything!" we had promised.

Sadly, that was his first and last Oesfees, but we hadn't missed one since, and even with me in London dealing with William's affairs, Patrick and Catherine were there to represent Alex.

The funeral director in London had put a small amount of William's ashes into a tiny urn for me to take back to South Africa. The bigger urn with his ashes would stay with Bart and Tracey until we could decide what to do. William had always felt a strong affinity for Scotland, so we were thinking of scattering his ashes somewhere suitable in Scotland, but in the meantime his ashes were safe with his friends in London. We decided to bury the small urn of William's ashes with Alex on the wine farm, and on a sunny afternoon in March 2016, Patrick, Catherine and I made the sad walk through the beautiful forest of trees, along the riverbank, to Alex's Tree, where we had buried Alex's ashes in January

2009. Seven years and two months after that day, we buried the small urn of William's ashes with those of his beloved brother.

As we were walking back to the car I had a very strong sense of William's presence, and I was sure I could feel his expression of thanks and satisfaction. When I mentioned this to Patrick and Catherine, they told me they had also sensed his presence, and they had also had the feeling that he was saying thank you for bringing him to the place where Alex was resting.

Two weeks later we had a big gathering in our home theatre to celebrate William's life. We had extended an open invitation to friends and family to join us in celebration of his life, and we were overwhelmed by the number of friends and family who came. For the evening I had made a slideshow with photographs of William from babyhood to adulthood and put it on a DVD, and throughout the evening a collection of photos showing a laughing baby William with just one tiny tooth in his mouth, a toddler with a dimpled cheek, a small boy with twinkly eyes, and a teenager and young adult, silently looped on our large screen, as we raised our glasses and drank a toast to his life and in his memory. There were no speeches, and no formalities, only the warmth and kindness of friends and family.

CHAPTER 13

Quite naturally and inevitably life moves on, and people move on too, because they have their own lives to live, and their own highs and lows to deal with. But what we did not expect was the change of attitude towards us. Suddenly, people who had known us for many years avoided us in public and scuttled past without acknowledging us. One evening we were having a pizza in one of our favourite eating places when I saw a couple sitting a few tables away from us. We had known them for many years, and their son had been one of William's best friends throughout their primary school days. They had lost their daughter several years earlier, and after Alex died we also shared that unfortunate bond. Through the years, whenever we bumped into them while out shopping, they always stopped for a chat. But that evening in the restaurant they clearly tried to avoid us by averting their eyes and keeping their heads down, and as soon as they had paid, they rushed past without greeting us. This happened again a few weeks later when we saw friends sitting a few tables away from us in a different restaurant. Like the previous couple, they also pointedly ignored us, but as they left the woman silently mouthed, "I'm sorry" as they hurried away.

A few weeks later I joined Patrick for drinks in the bar at his workplace. When I arrived Patrick was standing with a group of his colleagues, most of whom I had known very well for many years, so I joined him in the group, but within a few minutes the small gathering had almost imperceptibly shifted, and we were no longer included. We were standing alone, outside the group. This happened so many times, in so many different places, and in so many different ways, that we eventually came to expect it, but it was very hurtful and difficult to be shunned in such a way.

Fortunately there were some exceptions when friends or acquaintances did make the effort to approach us and talk to us. One evening we were at a function when we spotted a couple we had known for many years, standing in a small group of people. We fully expected them to ignore us, but as soon as everyone started to filter into the venue they hung back, and before we followed the crowd in, they stopped us to talk about what had happened to our family, and to express their sadness about our loss. It didn't happen often, but when it did these moments of kindness and thoughtfulness meant a great deal to us during those dark days.

When it came to meeting close friends in a social setting, it was also difficult. We had been members of the same small wine club for about thirty years, and we all knew each other very well, but the one topic that nobody wanted to touch on was the death of William, and how we were coping with it. We found that quite hard to deal with, but when it came to more casual friends it was even worse. Patrick and I had lived in Port Elizabeth for over forty years and naturally we knew many people. It was a standing joke in our wide circle of friends that one only needed to go to the local shopping mall, Walmer Park, to see someone you knew. A simple shopping expedition would invariably take much longer than planned because there was always someone to stop and chat to.

For me that all changed in March 2016. People who had known me for decades, and whose children had grown up with our children, started to duck and dive when they saw me in the food aisles or in the mall. Some dashed past me, trying to pretend they were in a rush and hadn't noticed me, and others mumbled a quick "hi" as they scurried away. Very, very few stopped to talk to me, and it soon became clear that I was a pariah, and someone to be avoided.

Eventually I found that the only way to get through any grocery shopping was to park my car far away from the mall entrance, fetch a shopping trolley, and keep my eyes down all the way into the supermarket and during my shopping, only looking up briefly to get what I needed and check where I was going. Keeping my head down meant I didn't have to see anyone or see the look of panic in their eyes as they tried to avoid me. Very often, when Patrick returned from work in the evenings I would tell him about yet another supposed friend who had deliberately ignored me, and it never ceased to hurt us that people we had known for more than half our lives could turn away at such a time. But they did, and it was very painful. I cannot deny that it made an already very difficult time so much worse. Those experiences have made me question the long-term value of friendships and the sincerity of those we think we know. Do true and enduring friendships really exist? Or do they wither when times are tough? That certainly was my experience, and it has altered my view on friendship forever.

But there were some very dear people who did show friendship and kindness, and I will always value and appreciate what they did, because it meant a great deal to me. They were in the minority, but they were there.

CHAPTER 14

After completing her TB treatment, and after being given the TB clearance certificate from the Cape Town radiologists, Catherine could finally apply for her ancestral visa. This time her application was successful, and two months after William's tragic death, she was back in London, living in our house in Cricklewood. It was not easy saying goodbye to her as, understandably, both Patrick and I felt very anxious about her going back on her own, to the house where had William died. But she was adamant that she was not going to change her future plans because of what had happened. She had studied a BA Honours in English Literature and Creative Writing at Middlesex University, and she wanted to find a job as a teacher's assistant for a year or two and then consider doing a Master's Degree in English Literature. Remaining in South Africa was not an option for her. She enjoyed living in London, and she also felt uncomfortable living in a country like South Africa with such a high level of violent crime. She wanted to return to London, and we were not about to stand in her way, despite our reservations.

Regardless of what had happened, Catherine was happy to be back in London, and she seemed to be coping fairly well under the difficult circumstances. But the reality was that she was very much alone, because she had not made any friends during her three years at university. She had never been keen on clubbing or partying, and that was what most young people did in London over weekends, so Catherine wasn't a part of the student social scene. She preferred a quieter life, and when she still had her brother as company it did not bother her much that she didn't have friends. But now all that had changed for her.

A short while after her arrival in London she decided to apply for a dog walking job to earn some money and to give herself the chance to get out and about at the same time. She made several applications, and received a few requests for interviews, but none of the dog walking jobs materialised, which made her feel quite despondent and isolated. We were worried about her all the time, but all we could do was keep in daily contact to try and keep her spirits up, from a distance.

As most South Africans would know, the scourge of violent crime is rife throughout the entire country, and several of our friends and family have been victims of either violent muggings or of serious assaults during house robberies. We had been fortunate up to that point, but we were living behind high walls, with locked doors and burglar bars, with alarms around the garden and inside our house, always vigilant and aware that we lived with the risk of being the next victim, and this made Catherine very anxious about us. She wanted me to keep in touch on WhatsApp all the time, and she was particularly worried when she knew we were not at home. The possibility of leaving South Africa and settling in the UK had been on my mind for a long time, even before we were faced with the difficult situation we now found ourselves in, but Patrick had made it clear that he was not interested at all. Any suggestions by me that we should consider moving to the UK were met by the same reply: "It is just not possible or practical". As time went by, and as I had to deal with daily messages from Catherine checking up on me because she was anxious about us, not to mention my concerns about her being alone in London, I became determined that, sooner rather than later, we would have to move. I was not prepared to continue the way we were, with Catherine so far away, with her feeling constantly anxious about us and with us feeling constantly anxious about her. And the fact that I was being shunned or ignored by so many people made me even more keen to leave.

But regardless of what I believed we should do, we were stuck in a stalemate because Patrick was simply not prepared to consider moving to the UK. He had a very successful practice as an advocate, and he was well settled in his life in Port Elizabeth. Naturally the thought of giving it all up for an unknown future was too difficult for him to contemplate. And so, as the days, weeks and months dragged by, we hobbled along trying to get through life as best as we could. At least I could take comfort from the thought that we would be back in London at the end of June to visit Catherine, because we were planning to do another one of our Animal Anti-Cruelty League fund-raising walks in England. This was something we had done annually since 2011, to raise funds primarily for the sterilisation of dogs and cats in impoverished townships around Port Elizabeth, and in 2016 we were planning to walk the South Downs Way, which starts in Winchester and ends in Eastbourne.

A few weeks before we arrived in London Catherine decided that she would like to get a dog to keep her company, and she spent a great deal of time contacting animal shelters to find a suitable dog. But at the same time, she was also trying to find work as a teacher's assistant, and this was an obstacle to her adopting a dog, because the rules of dog adoption are very specific in the UK. Dogs may not be adopted by anyone who is away from home for more than four hours a day, without them showing that they had a signed contract with a dog walker. If Catherine did find a job, she would most certainly be away from the house for more than four hours a day, and dog walkers do not come cheap, so she would not be able to afford that. When we arrived in London she told us about the difficulties she was experiencing in adopting a dog, and we offered to ask friends who lived outside London if they knew of any puppies which may be available from places other than animal shelters, but unfortunately that option also ended without success. It seemed that there would be no way for her to adopt a dog to be her companion, and she was very disappointed about it.

We left London to start our walk along the South Downs Way, promising Catherine that we would keep in regular contact on WhatsApp, because we knew she was lonely. Despite us trying to be positive about things, and sending regular messages, it was clear that Catherine was feeling quite despondent about her situation, and we didn't know what to do to help her feel better about things. One day as we were walking along one of the high ridges, I suddenly had a thought that perhaps she should give up on the idea of having a dog and consider adopting a kitten instead, and as soon as we were within an area where my phone had reception, I sent her a short message: "What about a kitten? It won't need to go for walks".

I didn't have to wait long before my mobile phone pinged back with her reply: "Yes, I think that is a great idea!"

Less than two hours later I received a WhatsApp photo of a kitten who was up for adoption at the RSPCA. "I think this is the one for me", Catherine's message read. It was a lovely little tortoiseshell/tabby kitten, and I replied immediately with, "She is perfect".

The kitten was duly booked, and Catherine decided to name her Ada. That same day she went out to 'Pets at Home' and stocked up on kitten food, a litter tray, cat litter, and toys for her new kitten. All she needed to do was to wait for our return to London, and then we would all go together to collect Ada. From that moment on it was clear that her spirits were lifted by the pending arrival of a kitten in her life, and at last she had something to look forward to.

The day after we returned from our long walk of the South Downs Way we arranged with the RSPCA to collect Ada, and with happy anticipation we set off on what turned out to be a very lengthy bus ride. The RSPCA was a long way outside London, and our journey was not made any shorter by us missing our stop and having to walk a fair distance, but eventually we arrived at the animal shelter. As soon as Catherine entered the kitten enclosure and knelt down to greet the little kitten, Ada walked over and greeted her with a tiny meow, and then she climbed onto her lap. They bonded instantly.

CHAPTER 15

All too soon it was time for us to say goodbye to Catherine and Ada and return to South Africa. I was dreading our departure because the thought of returning to a situation I no longer wanted to be in, and living in a place I no longer wanted to live in, was quite overwhelming. On the way to the airport I sat staring out of the taxi window, my mind far away from reality, as I wondered how I was going to face the future back in Port Elizabeth. All I knew was that I didn't want to be there. But regardless of how badly I wanted to move to the UK, the bottom line was that Patrick was not prepared to contemplate such a huge upheaval. We had a home in Port Elizabeth, he had his career as an advocate, we were very established, and to relocate would simply be too huge a step to take.

Although Patrick appreciated all the difficulties of us being so far away from Catherine, and he understood how hard it was for me to be shunned by people I thought were my friends, he simply could not see his way around giving up his career, selling up and leaving. And so, for a few more miserable months the two of us lurched along like wounded birds, not quite knowing what to do. Or perhaps it would be more accurate to say we did know what to do, but we were unable, or too afraid, to make the decision to do it. At the same time, Catherine was finding it hard to be alone every day and she was emotionally fragile. Ada was a good little companion, but Catherine still struggled at times, and it didn't help that we were so far away.

Because I have British Citizenship and a British passport, I started researching the possibility of Patrick getting a spousal visa. The good news was that he was eligible for it, and we would most likely be able to satisfy the very strict requirements to successfully apply for the visa. Theoretically speaking, even if we *did* have to jump through countless high hoops to get it, it was at least possible for us to do so if we could just make that final decision to sell up, pack up, and move. By this time I was already spending many hours every day looking for affordable houses in London, but it soon became clear that houses in London are very expensive, and eventually I started to look for properties further afield in smaller villages away from London. All this time I kept my plans to myself, hoping that eventually Patrick and I could come to a mutual agreement about the future.

By September our anxiety levels had become unbearable. We were both struggling to sleep, lying awake night after night, agonising over what to do, and all the time we had our daughter in London who was permanently worried about us every time we left the house, just as much as we were permanently worried about her. We all knew only too well how fleeting life could be, and how easily things could change. One evening I was sitting in the kitchen with Patrick while he was preparing dinner, and at the same time I was communicating with Catherine on WhatsApp. She was coping quite well, but I knew it was not easy for her. After a few messages back and forth I received a message from her that was the final turning point for me.

It read: "Mom, life is too short for us to be so far apart".

She was right, and I made my mind up there and then to do something about our situation. Patrick was standing at the butchers' block in our kitchen, chopping vegetables for our dinner, and I read her words to him. He listened intently, but carried on chopping vegetables in silence.

"She is right, life is too short to be so far apart, and we either go together, or I go alone, but I am going", I told him.

He carried on chopping for a few seconds, and then he paused, looked at me and replied.

"I know we have to move and be closer to Catherine, but I don't want to live in London, I want to go to Arran", he said.

It took my brain a few moments to process what I had heard, because I had never even considered Arran as a possibility. In fact, I had hardly even thought about Arran again since our two-night visit there in January 2015. But Patrick went on to tell me that he had such a strong and definite sense of wanting to move to Arran that he would be prepared to sell up, give up his career and go, if I would agree to living on Arran. Finally, after all the miserable months of agonising over our situation, Patrick had reached the point where he was prepared to move. The idea certainly took me by surprise, but I needed no persuading whatsoever and within minutes I had my laptop on the table, searching for properties on Arran. We were both glued to the laptop screen, dinner almost forgotten, as we went from properties on Arran to YouTube videos about Arran, and then to whatever else we could find on the internet about the island. At long last we started feeling that there was a way ahead, and the more we looked for information on Arran, the more we liked what we saw. After all, if we were going to make a change, we may as well make it a proper change. And what could be better than moving to a beautiful island off the west coast of Scotland?

It was all good and well for us to feel excited, but there was one other person who needed to be consulted about the plan. We obviously had to ask Catherine how she would feel about it because after all she would have to be happy with our choice if we were going to make the move to be together.

One of our main reasons for planning the move was to be closer to her, so her approval was vital to any future plans.

Without wasting any time, I phoned her and asked her how she would feel about moving to the Isle of Arran with us. There was a moment's silence from her side, and when she replied she didn't sound overly thrilled at all.

"The Isle of Arran? What do you want to do on an island?" she asked me with a hint of disbelief in her voice.

"Well, Dad and I think it will be a good place to live", I replied, hoping for a little bit more enthusiasm. She wasn't entirely convinced about our supposedly bright idea, even after I tried to tell her how lovely it would be on Arran.

"But Mom, it won't help romanticising things you know. We have to be realistic", was her response.

She was right of course. Moving to an island may not be the most realistic thing to do, but we thought it would be the best thing to do under our circumstances. After all, what did we have to lose?

Catherine didn't sound too keen at all, so I suggested she go online to see what she could find out about Arran. After all, we had just spent quite some time finding information on the internet, and there was an abundance of it available, as well as many videos on YouTube. A few hours later I received a Skype message from her. "Okay. I am on board with your plan. I checked online and they have good vets on Arran, including an avian vet. It's fine, I agree. Although I have no idea what I am signing up for". Short and sweet. But she was on board.

She clearly had her priorities straight, because according to her, if there were good vets, it would be fine. She had a valid point, because living on an island was one thing, having quick access to a vet was important, although I will confess, I hadn't thought of that yet. And as things turned out, it was just as well there were good vets on the island, because down the line we would need a vet much sooner than we thought.

We were very relieved that she was prepared to come with us and give it a try, even if she did say she didn't know what she was signing up for. It was most certainly a proverbial leap into the unknown for us, with many risks attached. But despite this, it was as if a huge weight had been lifted from our shoulders once we finally made that decision, and after the long, dark months we could start talking about some kind of future again.

We knew it would be a massive undertaking if we wanted to pull it off successfully, and Catherine certainly wasn't the only one who didn't know what she was signing up for. None of us knew what we were signing up for, but we were determined to make every effort to pull off our epic move, and then we were going to do everything we could do to make it work. What else was there for us to do? We couldn't continue the way we were.

Moving lock, stock, and barrel, plus a veritable 'Noah's Ark' of pets, to a small island, where we had spent two nights as visitors and had never thought of visiting again, was quite a leap of faith if nothing else, but we were at rock bottom and as far as we were concerned, the only way to go after that was up. We had nothing to lose, and hopefully we would have something to gain.

That same night I sent Derrick and Carly a long email explaining what we had decided to do, and I gave them the reasons why we felt we had no choice. I wanted to give them the time to digest the news and have time to think about it first before we spoke about it. After all, it would affect them as well and we needed to know how they felt about our plans. But the very next day they both replied that they fully supported our plans, they understood our reasons, and they hoped everything would work out well.

It was only after we had come to an agreement on where we would go that Patrick told me a strange story. He said during the time I was in London dealing with everything after William had died, he kept hearing a voice in his head saying: "You need to go to Arran". At the time he thought it was so bizarre that he didn't mention it to me after I returned home. He quite simply put it out of his mind entirely. After all, he had no intention of going anywhere at all, let alone to an island off the coast of Scotland. But he told me the voice had been quite persistent, and he heard it repeatedly for several days: "You need to go to Arran".

Is it too fanciful to believe that Alex was sending him a message? Or William? Or was this message coming from his subconscious? The answer will very much depend on the individual belief of each person. It doesn't really matter either way, what did matter was that Patrick had this very definite message, and he initially ignored it because he thought it was too nonsensical to even contemplate, let alone mention to anyone.

CHAPTER 16

Once we had finally made our decision, and the thought was out in the open between us, we started our plans in earnest. And there were a great many plans to be made. From that moment onwards we had a tacit understanding that Patrick would inform his colleagues and start dealing with all the many documents and mountains of files from his years as an advocate, as well as all things relating to his Chambers. And I would start the process involving the relocation of our pets to the UK, the process of applying for Patrick's visa, and the huge task of clearing and sorting through things which we had accumulated together as a family over almost three decades in our family home. My plan was to take it room by room, shelf by shelf, drawer by drawer and cupboard by cupboard, and I knew it would be a mammoth task sorting and clearing things out that we would not be taking with us, with the main aim of getting each room ready for the day we would finally have to pack up. It would be a major effort, and we both spent every day with just one single focus - ticking the boxes we needed to tick to make our move to Arran a reality. There were difficult moments, such as when I had to sort through a box of baby shoes from each of our four children, remembering the little feet that had worn, and shaped, those shoes. Sorting through the many little pictures drawn by toddler or children's hands brought back many memories, and I found myself at times hugging their old baby garments before I could put them into the boxes ready to go to a charity shop. Tough decisions had to be made. I had so many keepsakes from their baby and childhood days and my natural instinct was to keep everything, but I knew that it would be impossible. It was not the time to be emotional about anything, there was far too much that needed to be done. After months of wishing and hoping that we could make that big decision to pack up and leave it was finally happening, and I had to get on with the job at hand without getting bogged down by my sentimentality and sadness. Every day I chose one room, and my day's job was not done until the selected drawers and cupboards were all sorted and cleared, ready for removal day. The Bargain Box charity shop in Walmer almost ran out of space with the carloads of clothes, books, toys, and household goods that I dropped off each day, but no matter how much I took away, there was so much more.

Patrick faced the same huge task at work every day, sorting and clearing. He had mountains of paperwork and documents to go through, he had to arrange the sale of his large collection of Fred Page paintings, as well as his vast collection of Law Reports and many other law books and journals, and he had many arrangements to make regarding his work and his Chambers. One of our trickiest problems was what to do with all the papers we needed to dispose of. Some papers could be put into our recycling bin, but there were many that needed to be shredded, specifically the papers and confidential documents relating to Patrick's legal briefs through the years. We tried burning the papers, but that would have taken us months! And shredding by hand would take just as long, if not longer. Fortunately, our problem was solved by a company who collected the papers for shredding, and even paid a small amount for it, so that was the perfect solution to a tricky problem. It is one thing stashing piles of paperwork and documents away in cupboards and filing cabinets 'for another day'. But disposing of them when 'another day' finally arrives is an entirely different ball game.

CHAPTER 17

Dealing with the relocation of our pets was my responsibility, and I started to put the arrangements into place the day after we had made the decision to move to Arran. We were very lucky to have a pet relocation agency in Port Elizabeth, and I contacted them to get all the requirements for taking pets into the UK. The list was daunting to say the least, but Move-a-Pet is highly professional and I was assisted every step of the way as I navigated the rules and regulations of relocating pets from South Africa to the UK. Thank goodness the quarantine rules are no longer in place, provided certain specific requirements are met, and very soon after contacting Move-a-Pet we knew our pets were going to be in the very best of hands. They always responded quickly to any of my queries, and I certainly had many. I will confess right here and now that I am a paranoid pet parent, and yet they were more than understanding. They kept me up to date on developments and made sure that I did everything that needed to be done within the correct time frame.

The first thing we needed to do in the process of getting our pets ready for relocation was to take the two dogs and the three cats to our vet. They all had to have the Titre Test, which tests for rabies antibodies. The test results would take several weeks, so the sooner we had the tests done, the sooner we would have the results, and the sooner we could continue with our relocation plans for them. Anyone who has tried to get one cat, let alone *three* cats, into a cat carrier for a trip to the vet will know how diabolically difficult that can be. How do the little blighters know what we are planning to do? At the first sight of the cat carriers they vanished into the darkest corners of our large house, and no amount of calling or cajoling brought them forth. It took searching from room to room, often on hands and knees to round them up, and after rounding them up, we had to do battle with three very determined and furious four-legged felines to get them into their cat carriers. We were dripping in sweat even before we left for the vet! At least dogs are so much easier to trick into the car, and Percy was not at all worried when we put his lead on. Of course, little Mia, being the tiniest Yorkie, just needed to be picked up and carried to the car. But the cats gave us a good run for our money.

The vet had to draw blood, check their microchips, and record everything for each pet very meticulously, because the microchip number and the blood sample for each pet obviously had to match. The word 'bedlam' entered my mind as we worked our way through them all. Somehow, I think the vet felt the same, because at one point I heard him muttering, "I think you are crazy to be doing this". He was referring to our plans to move to Scotland, of course. Did we think we were crazy? Well, not entirely crazy. But it did take a small measure of craziness to do what we were doing, I will admit. Such a decision can probably not be made by anyone who is entirely sane. But after what we had gone through, I am not sure that we were entirely sane at that time anyway.

The decision to take our two parrots was not an easy one to make. We were worried about the long flight and the general stress they would endure along the way. At one point we debated the wisdom of taking them, and we asked Derrick and Carly if they would take them in if we felt we didn't want to put them through the long journey. They were more than willing to have Riley and Paulie if we decided to leave them, but as much as we were worried about how they would cope during their long flight, we dearly love them, and we didn't want to leave them. Eventually Patrick and I decided to ask one of our vets, who is an expert on birds. I phoned her and explained our fears and concerns, but she reassured me that they would be fine, and she said that if they were her birds, she would not hesitate to take them. Her opinion very much set us at ease, and it took a heavy weight off our minds to know we would not need to say goodbye to them when we left. With that decision settled, the next step was to have the parrots microchipped, which was a new worry for us. This procedure requires general anaesthetic, because the chip needs to be implanted deep into the breast muscle of parrots to prevent the birds from picking at it afterwards. Naturally we were anxious about the procedure, and Patrick and I spent the entire day worrying about them, until the receptionist phoned and told us that everything had gone well, they were both very chipper, and we could fetch them. When we arrived at the vet surgery we could hear Paulie's ear-piercing screeches, and we knew she was very much back in form. The receptionist and the vets were laughing at her antics, commenting on her cheeky personality. They may have been laughing, but I am sure they were happy to see her go. She truly is a little green imp, always trying to be funny and cheeky, and she has a very loud screech indeed. Riley on the other hand is a thinker. He watches everything around him, learning new words in context, and easily imitates our voices and what we say. We were very happy that we did not need to face the prospect of leaving them behind, although if it was the safer option, of course we would have done so. But thankfully that would not be necessary.

Through the years I had always been very particular about getting our pets vaccinated regularly, and that included the rabies vaccine, so I knew the Titre tests would probably indicate that they had the required level of rabies antibodies, but it was still a rather anxious wait until we got the results because if they did not meet the requirements, it would seriously delay our plans. Fortunately that worry was dispelled when we got the results back and it showed they were all within the expected levels as far as rabies antibodies went. Once the Titre tests were done and the results were back, and as soon as the parrots had been microchipped, the pets all had to be booked on flights to Edinburgh. Most days I felt as if I was running around in a circle chasing my own tail, because we still had so many hoops to jump through and we had no certainty at all about a workable time frame. Quite a few of the decisions we had to make were a complete leap into the dark, with us hoping for the best that everything else would fall into place. Booking flights for the pets was not as simple as one would expect. There were rules and regulations about when and how pets could be flown from one country to another, and at that stage we didn't even have our own departure dates. The entire sequence of events would have to be very specific, and we hadn't even started on it yet. All we had done was make our decision to move to Arran, and we had started the process to get our pets ready to join us. We hadn't remotely scratched the surface of officialdom at that point.

Our biggest worry was that we didn't know when, or even if, Patrick would be able to leave South Africa, because he still had to apply for his visa, but before he could apply for his visa, we needed to show we had somewhere to live. Without proof of fixed accommodation he had no chance of getting his visa. To buy a house on Arran, we would first have to sell our house in London, but Catherine was still living in the house in London, so naturally we didn't want to sell the house and buy a house on Arran until we were sure that Patrick would actually get his visa. What if we sold the house and everything fell flat, leaving Catherine without a roof over her head? It was like the age-old question: 'What comes first, the chicken or the egg?'

Not having things neatly arranged, well organised, and properly in place is one of my big bugbears, but I had to change my attitude on that very rapidly. There was absolutely no certainty in any of our plans, nothing was easy to organise or arrange, and there was going to be a whole lot of leaping into the dark and hoping for the best, as we tried to navigate completely unknown territory.

In so many instances we felt we were constantly having to put the proverbial cart before the horse, and it was nerve-wracking. Until we had the two parrots, the three cats and our two dogs booked on flights, Move-a-Pet could not start processing their upcoming relocation. But Patrick still didn't have his visa, and we had no fixed address yet. And so, the 'circular tail chasing' just seemed to go on and on. Keeping our fingers crossed, Mia, the Yorkie, and the three cats were tentatively booked on a flight due to leave South Africa on 15 March, although we would ultimately have to take into account the specific regulation that pets entering the UK had to arrive within five days of their owners. We decided to worry about that closer to the time, and we held back on Percy's booking because we couldn't fly more than four pets on one flight. We decided that we would book him on the same flight as the parrots, whenever that may be.

The relocation of our parrots was much more difficult. Apart from the paperwork required to relocate them, Riley is an African Grey, which is on the CITES list of endangered species, and getting all the required documents together for him was quite a challenge. One of the requirements for transporting parrots across international borders by plane is that they have to be booked on the exact same flight as their registered owner, which in our case is Patrick. This rule is to try and stop the illegal sale and export of parrots, and of course it is to be welcomed. But it did make things rather difficult for us because we didn't know when, or even if, he would get his visa. Once again, we had no choice but to go ahead and book Patrick, Percy the dog, and the two parrots on a flight from Port Elizabeth to Edinburgh for 16 April, and hope for the best. By then we were getting used to the thought that everything was a case of 'hoping for the best'.

CHAPTER 18

The process of applying for a spousal visa is an absolute minefield, and I quite simply did not feel confident enough to deal with it, so we appointed an immigration agent. He was very competent at his job, and it was a huge relief for me to leave it in his hands. It certainly wasn't a cheap option, but at least it was one thing less to get too stressed about, although obviously the visa was a huge source of concern to us.

Not everyone thought we were doing the right thing by giving up our home and everything else in Port Elizabeth and moving to an island off Scotland. We could almost hear the buzz in our ears as our decision was discussed behind our backs, and many heads were most certainly shaking in disapproval. One day a friend and colleague of many years called Patrick into his chambers and told him that we were making a very big mistake. He said moving was not the solution and suggested we should rather go for counselling. And the same thing happened to me, when a friend of long standing invited me for tea, which was quite a surprise because we had known each other for many years, and she had never invited me for tea before. It soon became clear why she had extended the unexpected invitation when, after some small talk, she steered the conversation towards the benefits of us going to therapy, rather than us giving up everything and moving away.

Anyone who hasn't faced the aftermath of the death of two of their children may find it easy to think everything will be solved through counselling, but that idea is very misguided. Some things can never be helped or healed by counselling or therapy. And how could anyone else possibly know about our feelings, or about our life as it had become?

We knew we didn't need or want counselling, because even if we spent the rest of our lives going to counselling, it would never make us and our family whole again. And anyway, we didn't have to explain or justify our decision to anyone. It was ours to make, whatever the outcome.

Still, there were many times when the thought of what we needed to do became quite overwhelming, but we kept reminding ourselves, and each other, that we just needed to keep level heads and do what we needed to do. In those difficult and stressful times, our main mantra became: "We *have* to make this work. It will be worth all the stress and trouble", and each evening we would toast our daily victories, some of them very small and some of them quite big.

Day after day we kept going, through late September, through October and into November. Our house in London had been on the market for a few weeks already, and we finally put our house in Port Elizabeth on the market as well. Meanwhile I was spending many hours every day searching the internet for our new home on Arran, with a list of properties waiting for Patrick after work each evening. I had contacted an estate agent on the island who recommended that we personally view any properties we were interested in because it would be far too risky to buy anything without seeing it first. Naturally this made perfect sense, and we would plan a trip for viewing when we were in London in December. But for the moment we were just browsing and making a list of possible houses for us to consider, and in a way, we were also dreaming of a new start and something to look forward to in the future.

CHAPTER 19

By mid-November 2016, with our complicated plans gradually falling into place, we felt it would be best if I went to Catherine in London as soon as possible. There would also be a lot of sorting and clearing of cupboards and rooms to deal with in the Cricklewood house, and Catherine couldn't do that on her own, so we decided it would be a good thing if I went sooner rather than later. Fortunately, we had managed to sell the Cricklewood house in early November, but we would have to get rid of some of the furniture and household goods, and I still needed to clear out most of William's possessions. His career as a software developer meant that he had left a great deal of computer hardware as well computer related books and files behind. I had sorted through quite a lot of his things while I was in London eight months earlier just after he died, but there were still many boxes of papers, books, clothes, shoes, old computers and monitors, and other possessions to deal with.

As soon as I was back in London Catherine and I would be working our way through every drawer, cupboard and room, tidying and clearing out unwanted things. Catherine would focus on her own room, and I would deal with the rest of the house. It was going to take something close to military precision for us to pull off the mammoth task of sorting out and packing up two homes, and co-ordinating two moves. Not to mention the relocation of our pets. Fortunately, the house in Cricklewood was much smaller and the task was not as huge, but there was still a lot to do, and I decided to start with William's things.

At one point William used to sell goods on Amazon, and there were thirty boxes of brand-new battery-operated racing cars stacked in a cupboard which had not been sold. We were sure someone would have a use for them, but where did I even start with trying to get rid of them? Before I left Port Elizabeth Patrick suggested we take them to a Cash Convertors to try and sell them there, and with no other ideas on the matter, I agreed. Catherine was far less enthusiastic about the plan when I informed her, but in the absence of a better solution, she reluctantly agreed to help me. We packed the bulky boxes into two very large suitcases, a large carry-bag, and two backpacks, and set off for Wembley, on a cold and grey December morning.

Our little jaunt meant we had to haul this load on and off two separate buses, and walk quite a long distance to Cash Convertors, navigating the busy sidewalks of Wembley, dodging pedestrians and shoppers every step of the way. We were quite frazzled by the time we reached Cash Convertors and very keen to finally get rid of our load, but when I asked at the counter about the possibility of them taking the cars off my hands, the assistant took one look inside the cases and asked me for receipts. I explained that our son who had bought them had passed away, and I didn't know where the receipts were. Not surprisingly, the assistant said he was very sorry, but they could not buy the cars without any receipts. Our entire effort had been a spectacular waste of energy!

It sure was disappointing, but I could see their point. It probably looked very dodgy. I may have been disappointed, but Catherine was very annoyed with the whole situation, and she didn't hide her annoyance as we dragged all the cases and bags onto the two separate buses, to get back to Cricklewood. As we were sitting on the bus in London traffic, visions of the television series 'Only Fools and Horses' came to mind, and I jokingly said to Catherine, "That bloke probably thought we were trying to sell dodgy goods, like Delboy and Rodney from 'Only Fools and Horses'. Maybe he would have bought the cars if I told him that the boxes of cars had fallen off the back of a lorry?" My joke went down like a lead balloon, and I was met with a cold glare and a curt, "Well, I don't think it's funny!"

After a long silence, I suggested to Catherine that it may be worth trying our luck at the Cat Protection charity shop close to our house. We were certainly not taking them back home, and I couldn't see a charity asking for any receipts. With that settled we lugged everything off at the bus stop close to the charity shop, and when I opened the large suitcase of brand-new battery-operated cars and told the volunteer in the shop that we had thirty of them, he was delighted. After all, it was a few weeks before Christmas and he told us he was sure the cars would sell like hotcakes.

For a few weeks afterwards we used to see a small display of the cars in the charity shop window whenever we walked past, and they did indeed sell like hotcakes, with the sold cars being replaced by a new batch almost every day. But it tugged at my heart to see William's cars in the window, and I felt deeply sad at the sight because it was very hard to come to terms with what had happened. I consoled myself with the thought that since it was just before Christmas and they were selling quite fast, at least that would mean good money for the cat charity. We also took most of William's clothes, shoes and books to the same charity shop, and I was sure that William would have approved of what we were doing.

If the little racing cars posed a challenge, getting rid of the computer equipment was much more difficult. William had several old computer monitors, hard drives and bags of computer components stacked in a cupboard, and everything was big, heavy and bulky. We tried to dismantle what we could, and then we just stuffed smaller components into larger pieces to save space. But even so, we still had three large and very heavy suitcases and several heavy carry bags to get to the local Council recycling tip. Taking the bus with that load would be way too difficult, so I phoned a taxi. And even then, it was quite a task getting everything into the boot of the taxi. The taxi driver dropped us off at the entrance to the recycling tip and we lugged everything in, thanking our lucky stars that we hadn't taken a bus. Taking public transport in London with so many suitcases and bags would have been a nightmare.

At the recycling tip we had to climb quite a high set of steps to reach the top of the massive dumpsters and it took us many trips, up the steps and then down again, hauling heavy bags behind us, to dispose of everything. Load after load, we carried and pulled the bulging bags up the steps and dropped the contents into the dumpsters. It was exhausting, and it was a huge relief when we were finally done, but at the same time, having to dump so many of William's things in a dumpster was really tough. I felt like a traitor disposing of his things as if I didn't care, and I am sure Catherine felt the same. It was such a hard thing to do, but there was no point in dwelling on it. We had absolutely no choice.

After clearing out most of William's things we could finally start concentrating on the rest of the house, making sure we only kept what we would be taking with us. Meanwhile, Patrick was holding the fort back in Port Elizabeth, and dealing with the myriad of things he had to do. He was due to join us later in December for Christmas and New Year, and at least that was something we could all look forward to. Since the beginning of March 2016, when I had taken that phone call from Seth, it had been a most horrendous year. We were living in a nightmare, with the aftermath of

William's death and the complete disruption of our lives. Throughout the year Patrick and I had been apart very often, with him in Port Elizabeth trying to do his best to keep going, and me in London, being there for Catherine and dealing with everything that needed attention. We were looking forward to a few weeks together again, just to give us time to try and regain our equilibrium.

For the moment though, Catherine and I were very much immersed in packing up everything in the house, and our immediate problem was to find boxes. We found ourselves going around to local supermarkets and corner shops each day, asking for empty cardboard boxes, and in almost every instance we were kindly offered as many as we wanted. We filled the empty boxes every day, and went 'box hunting' every evening, and gradually we started seeing results, as the boxes stacked up on the one side of the living room, and the drawers, cupboards, and rooms became emptier.

Putting up our Christmas tree had always been a fun family event, especially for Patrick, who remained an eternal child at heart when it came to Christmas. When our children were young he used to pull out all the stops to create a magical Christmas experience for them, even putting baby powder on his shoes and leaving shoe prints across the carpet to the Christmas tree, to make the children believe Father Christmas had left his own prints the night before. He would make every effort to create Christmas magic for them during their childhood.

Over the years he had built up a collection of beautiful Christmas tree decorations, and he took great pleasure in decorating the tree every year, usually with the help of whichever offspring were there. But Christmas of 2016 was not a joyful time for us, and none of us felt the desire to put up a Christmas tree. It was hard to think that just one year ago William had, as usual, helped us put up the Christmas tree. The thought of doing it without him didn't bear thinking about, but as things turned out we had a handy excuse which saved us from making that difficult decision. Catherine's cat Ada was only a few months old, and it was very likely that she would create havoc in the tree and damage the decorations, so it was easy to use Ada as the reason for us not putting up our Christmas tree. To make a token effort, I brought out some tinsel and Catherine strung it along the curtain rails to create a little bit of a festive look. But other than that, we didn't have the heart to do anything more.

CHAPTER 20

Before Patrick was due to arrive in London for Christmas, we had discussed our plans to make a quick trip to Arran in search of our new home. Our London house was sold, and we needed to secure a house on Arran as soon as possible, otherwise Catherine would be left without a roof over her head when the new owners moved into the house in March. Time was going to be very tight from all perspectives because Patrick was arriving in London on 19 December, and we would have to travel to Arran the very next day, on 20 December. It would take us a day to get from London to Arran, we needed at least two days to view the list of houses we had in mind, and then it would take another day to get back to London. We wanted to be back in London by 24 December, to have time to stock up for the festive period, and to spend Christmas with Catherine, so we only had four days in total to get to Arran, view some houses, put in an offer on a house, and get back to London. That would be cutting things very fine indeed, but ever since we had taken the decision to make the big move we had been sailing pretty close to the wind most of the time anyway. And this was going to be no different.

When Patrick arrived in London on 19 December he was extremely tired after the seemingly endless weeks of stress and worry, so I told him to let me go through the home reports of the houses on our viewing list, while he relaxed and tried to unwind before going to bed. We would have an early start the following morning, and he was completely exhausted. The sooner he tried to switch off his mind and get some rest, the better.

After supper I settled at the computer and read through each of the fourteen home reports. Having the home reports beforehand is extremely useful, and I soon managed to whittle the list down from fourteen houses to just four. The rest had far too many negative reports, and we were certainly not going to take on any problems such as rising damp, leaking roofs, or dry rot. We had enough to worry about already. Having only four houses to choose from meant we were not exactly spoilt for choice, but we knew we simply *had* to select one of the four houses. There was no time for a second viewing.

It was a strange feeling setting off for Arran once again so soon after our first visit in January 2015, when we had travelled to Arran to meet Alex's friends. How could we ever have known that destiny would bring us back to Arran much sooner than we would ever have thought, under circumstances we could never have anticipated?

The train from Euston Station to Glasgow Central Station was packed with passengers, who were mostly making the trip to visit family for Christmas, and there was a happy atmosphere all the way, as they mostly looked forward to time with their families. My late mother was born on Christmas Day, and I have always believed that Christmas Day was a time for families to get together. Naturally, under the circumstances, I was reminded of how much our family had lost, with my mother long dead when she was only fifty-nine, our two sons gone in the short space of seven years, and any hope of future large family Christmas get-togethers, with children and new grandchildren, lost forever. But the jovial mood was all around us, and we soon got caught up in conversations, although I was hoping nobody would ask us where we were going or why. My answer, if I had the courage to be honest, would most definitely have put a damper on the atmosphere. It is something one learns quite quickly under these circumstances – the truth is sometimes too dreadful to share with others.

Our long train journey passed quickly, and before we knew it our train was pulling into Glasgow Central Station. We had a few hours to wait for the train to Ardrossan Harbour and to pass the time Patrick and I went to a pub at the station to fortify ourselves with food and a much-needed pint of ale. While we were sipping our drinks Patrick happened to look at the television above our heads, and I saw him prick up his ears. "Look at that", he said, pointing at the screen. It was the weather report, and it showed a storm approaching. It seemed Storm Barbara was making landfall across Scotland, and major travel disruptions were expected. We only had four days to get to Arran, find a house, and get back to London, and the last thing we needed was any form of travel disruption. We sat sipping our drinks in silence, trying to digest the latest development. At least the trains were still running on time, which was a good sign, so we crossed our fingers and hoped the travel disruptions would not affect us.

For the moment our luck held, and the train to Ardrossan pulled out of Glasgow Central as scheduled. We were feeling cautiously optimistic that we would get to Arran before Storm Barbara unleashed the worst of her fury, although we could hear that the storm was definitely gathering pace, and as the train went through Saltcoats a huge wave crashed over the sea wall and onto the train, causing our carriage to light up with an impromptu fireworks display, as the sparks flew around the train. Moments later the very jolly conductor came around and asked, "Did you enjoy the show?" with a big grin on his face. "Yes, quite spectacular!" we both replied, as we felt the train being buffeted around by the strong winds. By the time we arrived at Ardrossan Harbour, the wind was howling, the sea was raging, the rain was pelting down, and we were informed at the ticket office that the ferry to Arran was cancelled due to the storm. To say we were disappointed will be an epic understatement, but by then we had learned that we had to take whatever came our way, and deal with it. After all, why should life be easy if it can be downright difficult? And as things stood that evening, we were stranded in the ferry terminal, with a few fellow travellers, as Storm Barbara did her best to add more stress to our already frayed nerves. The staff at the ticket office were very helpful and they phoned a taxi to whisk us off to a guesthouse in Ardrossan. The weather was absolutely wild as our host dashed out to the taxi and shouted above the noise of the storm for us to follow her inside. Our room turned out to be large and luxurious, with a beautiful bathroom including a jacuzzi, but we were too exhausted and stressed to enjoy any form of luxury. All we wanted was a meal, with a few glasses of wine, and then some rest. Patrick spotted a supermarket out of the window and bravely set off in the foul weather to get us some wine, and after he returned, we ordered a delicious take-away meal, which we ate in the guest kitchen, making instant friends with our fellow stranded passengers.

As I lay in bed that night listening to the beating rain and the howling wind, all kinds of unpleasant scenarios kept running through my mind. What if we couldn't get to Arran and find a house before everyone closed down for Christmas and New Year? What would we do if we didn't have a house on Arran before Catherine had to vacate the house in Cricklewood? What if we managed to get over to Arran but couldn't get back in time to be with Catherine for Christmas, and she was left all alone? And just as worrying: What if Catherine and I got stranded like this when we were coming from London with her cat Ada and her two budgies? Or when Patrick and I had to bring our own pets across from Edinburgh after their arrival from South Africa?' Where would we stay with animals if we were stranded?

These worst-case scenarios ran riot through my head all night, as I tossed and turned for hours, and the high-pitched sound of tinnitus in my one ear grew ever louder, as it had been doing whenever I became very stressed. The long, dark night dragged on as I lay in bed listening to the raging storm outside, which was not showing any signs of abating, and I don't think I nodded off for more than an hour because I was so worried. But when morning dawned grey, wet, and cold, we arrived at the ferry terminal to be informed that the ferry was sailing. We both felt like dancing for joy as we made our way onto the ferry, and soon we were on our way to Arran to look for our new home.

We started our house viewing in Lochranza, although I had made it clear to Patrick that I was not keen to live that far north on the island. It seemed too remote for me, with very few amenities, but we decided to view the house anyway. The next two houses were in Brodick and none of them were suitable, although one house had some potential if we could make a few changes to the garden to accommodate the pets. We had our dogs Percy and Mia to cater for, so a safely fenced lawn area was important, we had two parrots who needed a conservatory for their large cages and where they could be let out every day, and we had four cats, our three cats and Catherine's cat, who would need an area of garden that could be enclosed and made cat proof, to stop them from roaming and to keep them safe. And on top of that, it was very important to find a house that would suit not only us, but it also had to have appropriate space for Catherine to live. Our choice of house had a long and specific checklist, and we had only four to choose from, not to mention exactly one day to find something that ticked all those boxes, or at least most of them.

After viewing the first three houses Patrick and I went for lunch and discussed the advantages and disadvantages of each house. Overall, it seemed they all had far more disadvantages that advantages, and we weren't sure that any of them would be right for us, so our hopes were well and truly pinned on the last house. We simply *had* to put in an offer before returning to London because everyone would be closing down between Christmas and New Year, and the process of making an offer on a house and eventually taking occupation is a long and slow process. We didn't have any time to spare because Catherine needed a place to live before mid-March, and that was only three months away. Whichever way we did it, we simply had to secure a house before we left Arran, even if it meant a few compromises to our checklist.

But we still had one house to view, and we were very much hoping that it would be suitable for us. After lunch we were back at the estate agents' office, and we set off with her to view this last house, which was in Whiting Bay. As the agent drove us through Lamlash and then on to Whiting Bay we were each deep in our own thoughts. It had been a harrowing year for us so far, with almost no let up at all, and the stress and anxiety of the past few months was starting to wear us down. What if the last house on the list was not suitable?

As the car pulled into the driveway, we noticed that the property was large, with more than enough space to create a safe garden area for the dogs and the cats, and we already knew from the photos online that the house had a large conservatory where the parrots could be kept. That already ticked some important boxes for us, and we were keen to view the interior of the house to see the layout, and to find out if it would cater for us as well as for Catherine. We had barely crossed the threshold when Patrick looked at me and said, "I think this is it. What do you think?" We hadn't even looked any further than the little porch yet, but it felt right for us. Still, we did have to at least do a proper viewing of the house before coming to our final decision, so we took a good look around. The bedrooms, living room and kitchen were all much smaller than what we had back in Port Elizabeth, but compared to the other three houses we had viewed, this house was the most suitable, even down to a fully functioning and separate self-catering unit for Catherine on one side of the house.

Once we were back at the estate agent's offices, we wasted no time in putting in an offer, and we waited anxiously as the agent phoned the sellers, who were away on holiday. Much to our relief the offer was accepted, and barring any mishaps, we had our new home on Arran. On the one hand we were absolutely elated, and on the other hand we felt quite stunned that we had actually found a house, and our offer had been accepted. It was almost too good to be true.

That evening we both went to sleep feeling somewhat less stressed, keeping our fingers crossed that the ferry would be sailing the next morning because Christmas was two days away and we wanted to get back to Catherine in London. We were awake and dressed very early the following morning and we were given the good news by our host that the ferry was sailing. Storm Barbara was over her huff, the weather had settled, and we were soon on our way across the Clyde to the mainland. Before heading back to London though we had to stop off in Saltcoats to see our new solicitor, who was going to deal with the ins and outs of the purchase of our house. At our appointment the solicitor duly went through the necessary requirements and paperwork we had to comply with, and he assured us that if everything went according to plan, and he wasn't envisioning any serious complications, we would be able to take occupation of our house at the beginning of March. He offered to liaise with the solicitor in London, who was dealing with the sale of our house in Cricklewood, to make sure that the transfer of funds from that sale was co-ordinated with the exact time that we had to make the payment for our house on Arran. Things are done differently in England and Scotland, but it was our very good fortune to have excellent solicitors on both sides to deal with everything very competently and thoroughly. It made everything much less stressful.

Our plans were slowly but surely starting to fall into place for us, and although we still had many hurdles to clear before we reached our final goal, at least we were going forward at a steady enough pace.

After three very eventful days we arrived in London feeling tired but happy, and we were keen to show Catherine photographs of the house. There was so much to show her and tell her about the house and the garden, and the three of us huddled together as Patrick scrolled though the many photographs he had taken on his iPad. Catherine seemed quite pleased with what she saw, and she was thrilled when she heard that she would have one part of the house to herself, with her own private front door. We would be together under one roof, but we would have our part of the house and she would have hers. It was the perfect arrangement.

We had a quiet Christmas Day, trying to be as happy as we could, and trying to remain positive, but it was hard not to think back on the other Christmases we had been together around the same table, and William's empty chair was a sad reminder of happier Christmas times, now lost to us. And also, I couldn't help thinking about the first time we spent Christmas in our flat in Cape Town without Alex, and how difficult it had been for us to be happy as we faced the empty chair where he had sat for his last Christmas, and how William had struggled that day with the loss and absence of his brother.

CHAPTER 21

With our holiday in London coming to an end it would soon be time for us to return to South Africa and pick up where we had left off. The plans for our move were going well, both in South Africa and in the UK, but there were a great many loose ends, on both sides, that were not even close to being tied together yet. Patrick was going to spend the next few months working his way through what was still a formidable list of things that needed to be done in Port Elizabeth, but I was only going to be with him for a few weeks before returning to London, where I would help Catherine pack up our household goods, and make sure everything was ready for the removal company in March.

Before returning to South Africa we made one more brief trip to Arran to measure the sizes of all the rooms. Our new house was much smaller than our house in Port Elizabeth, and we realised that we would have to carefully select only what would fit into the house. It was going to mean making difficult decisions, and we had to have exact measurements to help us make up our minds on what we wanted to keep. If something wouldn't fit in, we couldn't keep it. There was no other way. We also measured the windows for curtains, because we had decided to adjust the curtains we already had in our Port Elizabeth house, and not waste money on new curtains. What we were learning, and learning fast, was that there are far more important things in life than having too many material possessions. It is so easy to become weighed down by material goods, and it happens so gradually that it becomes a complete part of our existence, until one day, events may force us to re-evaluate what life is all about, what is important, what we really do need and what we can discard. We now found ourselves in that position, and we had to adjust our thinking accordingly.

With only a verbal offer and acceptance in place, but nothing signed and sealed yet, we were still worried that things may go wrong at any time. Selling in England and buying in Scotland is not as simple as one would think. The dates for the transfer of payments and the handing over of keys for occupation, in London and on Arran, all had to be carefully coordinated. It was slow and heavy going, but all the wildly flapping loose strings were slowly being gathered together, and neatly tied, one by one.

Amidst this frenetic time, and a few days before we returned to South Africa in January 2017, we celebrated Catherine's birthday. As the three of us were enjoying our celebratory meal in a restaurant, a fox strolled past the window ever so casually. We were on the first floor of a shopping mall, in London, and yet the fox seemed quite familiar and relaxed about the layout of the mall, the escalators, the lifts, and presence of people. It seemed to be saying to us, "Life goes on, if you adapt", as it strutted past with its tail in the air. A mere two years earlier we had celebrated Catherine's 21st birthday in London by taking her and William to dinner at a restaurant and then to see the show 'The Book of Mormon', and that was the same year we had taken advantage of our longer stay in London to go and meet Alex's friends on the Isle of Arran. It was only two years before, and yet for us it was another lifetime, and another world, before our lives were irrevocably changed. But the reality is that Life does have to go on. We get dealt a hand of cards, and even if it is a lousy hand, we have to play the game as best we can to the very end.

The night before we left London and returned to South Africa, William's friend Bart brought the urn with William's ashes to us. He and Tracey had kept the ashes safely for us until we knew what we wanted to do with them. We knew William had a great fondness for Scotland, and I had asked a family member if we could bury his ashes in the grave of my maternal great-grandmother, who is buried in Cowdenbeath. At least that would be at a place where family was resting, so it seemed the best idea at the time. He had often spoken about visiting Scotland again, and we decided that we would take him back to Scotland. A place he loved. But once we knew we were moving to the Isle of Arran we decided to take the ashes with us, where we would make a final decision on what to do with them once we were settled.

CHAPTER 22

A few days after Catherine's birthday it was time for us to say goodbye to her and return to South Africa to resume the task of preparing for the move. For me it would be a short stay in Port Elizabeth because I was due back in London in late February, while Patrick would remain on his own to deal with sale of our house, the sale of much of our furniture and goods, and the winding down of all relevant matters at his Chambers. Our plan was for me to return to London on 21 February to help Catherine finish packing up in readiness for the removal company, who were booked to load our goods on 8 March, and then Catherine and I would set off for Arran the following day. I was very much hoping that there would not be any ferry cancellations which may affect the removal truck or us. By this time the endless worry and stress had aggravated the tinnitus in my ear, with the volume being a good gauge of the level of stress I was under. The higher my stress levels, the higher the pitch and the louder the volume. Sometimes it sounded like a full orchestra of cicadas in my head!

If everything went according to plan, Catherine and I would be in our new home in Whiting Bay on 10 March, and Patrick would join us a few days later, just before the arrival of our little Yorkshire Terrier, and our three cats, who were due in Edinburgh on 15 March. At the time of our relocation to the UK it was still a requirement that a pet owner had to arrive in the UK within five days of their pets, otherwise the animals had to spend six months in quarantine. In our case it would be Patrick, who was going to make a special trip to the UK for that reason, because I would be arriving in the UK in February, and that was outside the five-day limit.

That rule has now been relaxed, but even without that requirement, I would not have managed to drive a rental car from Ardrossan to Edinburgh, on roads I did not know, collect three large cat crates and a little dog, drive back to Ardrossan, and navigate everything onto the ferry and then onto the bus back to Whiting Bay on my own. After looking at it from every angle, we decided that Patrick would have to come to the UK to help with the collection of the pets, and once the cats and little Mia were safely on Arran, he would return to South Africa to oversee the packing up of our furniture and household goods in Port Elizabeth, which was going to take three full days.

We still didn't know if Patrick would get his spousal visa, but we had gone ahead and made all our plans anyway, hoping for the best. If nothing untoward happened he would be on the same flight to Edinburgh as our dog Percy and the two parrots, on the 20th of April. And hopefully that would signal the final leg of our long journey from the evening in September 2016, six months earlier, when we had decided to move away from Port Elizabeth in South Africa to the Isle of Arran, off the West Coast of Scotland.

But that was still in the future, and there were many more bridges to cross, which meant that as soon as we were back in Port Elizabeth neither of us had any time to waste before we got back into our 'list checking and box ticking' mode. Patrick's visa was still a constant worry and until he had his visa safely in his hands, we were on edge. As anyone who has applied for a visa will know, it is always a nerve-wracking experience. We had an excellent emigration agent, and that helped a lot, but everything hinged on that visa. Without it, all our plans would turn to dust.

My final three weeks in Port Elizabeth passed by in a haze of packing and clearing, and decision making on what we would keep, what we would give away, and what we would sell. Some decisions were easy to make, but some were very difficult. When it came to my three pianos, I had to choose which one to take and which two to sell. My pianos were special to me, and I never expected I would have to part with any of them. In the case of my baby grand piano, the decision was easy - I knew it would have to be sold, but the other two pianos were of great sentimental value to me. My Yamaha piano had been a part of my life since 1975 and I had spent many hours either playing it, or teaching my pupils on it, and all four our children had learned to play the piano on the Yamaha through the years. I had also played my one and only April Fool's Day prank on Alex on that same piano, when he was about ten years old. He had told me one day that nobody would ever catch him in an April Fool's Day prank, because he would be way too smart to be tricked. So, of course the challenge was on, and I had to try and trick him. While he was at school on the morning of 1 April, I spent quite a long time sticking random piano keys together with Sellotape, in a way that it was totally invisible to anyone sitting in front of the piano. This meant every time a piano key was played, two or three keys would go down at the same time. I was sure he was going to be well and truly tricked, and I didn't have long to wait.

It was always Alex's habit to head straight for the piano as soon as he arrived home from school, even before he sat down for lunch. On this day, as usual, he made a beeline for the piano when he got home, and I hovered in the kitchen preparing lunch, keeping one ear trained on the study, and trying not to laugh at what was to come. As soon as Alex started to play the piano it was more of a cacophony than any recognisable tune, as random keys were going down when they were not supposed to. After a few seconds of a dreadful racket there was total silence, with him obviously trying to figure out what was happening. And then he tried again, but the result was the same. Once again, he stopped playing in total puzzlement, followed by silence for a few moments. And then it dawned on him that he had been tricked, and I heard him yell, "Nooooo!! What have you done!?" I strolled in and said casually, "Ah, guess who is an April Fool after all?" The look on his face was classic. He was completely bemused and tried to figure out what I had done to the piano, but it took him quite some time to work that out, and we both had a good laugh as he finally conceded that he had been well and truly tricked on April Fool's Day. It would be very difficult for me to part with that piano. But at the same time, my other piano, an upright Ottobach, carried just as many happy memories of Alex and me playing Monty Python songs together, with us singing "I'm a Lumberjack", the "Philosopher's Song" and "Every Sperm is Sacred", as the two of us plonked our way through the songs in a rather badly improvised duet, and with Patrick singing along with us. Our laughter usually made playing or singing quite hopeless, but that never stopped us hacking our way through the tunes in fits of laughter.

For me, musical instruments are not mere pieces of furniture, they are more like family members with a history and a story to tell. And deciding which piano to keep and which to sell was a very difficult choice, but I finally settled on keeping the Ottobach because I felt I would be taking a small part of those special moments of laughter with me, and I wanted to hold on to those memories if possible.

CHAPTER 23

Having only three weeks left in Port Elizabeth to do whatever I needed to do before leaving for London meant the final count-down had well and truly started for me, and there was very little time to think of anything else. There was one exception though, and that was the Knysna Celtic Festival, which was due to take place on 18 and 19 February, just days before my departure. We were still members of the Algoa Bay Caledonian Pipe Band, and as usual the pipe band was going to participate in the Knysna Celtic Festival. This would be our last opportunity to play with the band, and despite the very inconvenient timing, we wouldn't miss it for anything. Not only that, Knysna is very close to where Derrick and Carly live, and with our time in South Africa getting shorter, and with so much that still needed to be done, we could participate in the festival, and visit them afterwards on the same weekend. They were coming to watch the massed pipes and drums in Knysna, but there wouldn't be much time to see them on the Saturday because we were piping, so we had arranged to visit them the next day for lunch and to say goodbye, before returning to Port Elizabeth. Saying goodbye for a few weeks or even a few months was one thing, but saying goodbye for an unknown number of years was a different thing altogether. Our family had already lost so much, and this was also a loss, albeit of a different kind, that we had to come to terms with. We were truly caught between a rock and a hard place – having to leave one child behind in South Africa to be with the other child in the UK.

Playing at the Celtic Festival was a bittersweet experience for us in February 2017, not only because it was the last time we would play with our band, but more than anything it was bittersweet because of the painful memory that the previous year when we had played at the festival, and while we were having a wonderful time, William was most likely already dead. And we did not know.

Two days after the festival in Knysna, on 21 February 2017, it was time for me to say goodbye to Patrick, to our pets, and to what had been our family home for almost thirty years. Saying goodbye to our two old dogs Shadow and Roxie was particularly hard. They were both too old and too frail to make the long journey to Arran. At sixteen, Shadow was blind and deaf, and she was ill with liver failure, and at eighteen, Roxie was very arthritic and in pain. They would both be going on their own journey across the Rainbow Bridge, so it would be my final goodbye to them. It was really tough for me to say that last goodbye, but I was sure William would be there to meet them. Especially his 'Shaddie', when she arrived, because I believe beyond any doubt that animals can and do join us in the spirit world. William and Shadow had loved each other so much in this life, and I was certain that their reunion would be a very happy one.

Naturally it was also difficult saying goodbye to our other pets, even if they were going to join us later. I was worried about how scared they would be during their long journey, and I was nervous about them travelling such a long distance without us. In a way, I also felt guilty, because they had no say in such a life-changing decision and yet it would affect them so much. But we would never leave them behind. They are all part of our family, and as much as we worried about how they would cope on the long journey, we would not consider leaving without them.

As I got ready to leave for the airport, I made the conscious decision *not* to take one last walk through the garden or through the house, and I made the conscious decision *not* to look back at anything as I walked to the garage, on my way to the car. I thought it would be best to not stop and reflect on such things, and to not dwell on the fact that I was leaving the place we had called home for almost three decades. The home where we had raised our four children, partied and danced until daybreak, made so many memories, and tried to remain standing in the face of two life-changing tragedies. There was absolutely nothing to be gained from looking back, and if I wanted to find any kind of hope or peace in the future, I would have to try and look ahead.

As Patrick drove me to the airport, I did my best not to think of anything other than my flight and of seeing Catherine again. That is where I was going, and that was what I forced myself to focus on. We had come so far, the end of our long journey was on the horizon, and there was no point in dwelling on anything negative.

Airport terminals hold many memories. In those departure and arrival halls, people will experience extreme joy and excitement, as well as extreme sadness and sorrow. We had passed through Port Elizabeth airport many times through the years, and I always felt the memories crowd back into my mind every time we were at the airport. I could recall the excitement we shared every time we set off on one of our holidays. Or the very happy moments when we welcomed loved ones for a visit, waiting in great excitement as they stood at the carousel watching out for their luggage. But with every joyous arrival, there would also be the inevitable sadness of waving goodbye again. And then there were the awful memories of us waiting in the airport terminal for our flight to Cape Town in 2009, to attend Alex's memorial concert. And the numb pain I felt as I said goodbye to Patrick in March 2016, before I boarded the plane to London, after William had died.

As Patrick and I stood side by side in the departure hall, we were rather overwhelmed by our situation. It felt surreal as the moments ticked by, ever closer to the time I would have to say goodbye to him and leave South Africa for a future we had decided on, but which was totally unknown to us. After many months of agonising, and then months of planning, it was time for us to take the next step of this journey. Patrick would continue with the arrangements in Port Elizabeth, and I would continue with the arrangements in London, and hopefully we would manage to co-ordinate and successfully pull off our big move and eventually meet up again in our new home on Arran.

My emotions were in a turmoil as we finally said goodbye. On the one hand I was relieved to be going, because the past few months had been a very isolated and lonely time for me, as friends seemed to vanish into thin air. Two people had dropped in at our house briefly to say goodbye to me during the short time I was still in Port Elizabeth, but only two, and only because I asked them to. Nobody else had. So I was happy that the day had come for me to leave.

However, when it came to my lack of visible friends, there was one exception, which I will always appreciate and cherish. Our dear friend Linda-Louise, a long-standing true and loyal friend, who kept in regular contact with us through the years and even more so after William died. She often sent me messages of encouragement and kindness, especially while I was in London dealing with arrangements for William's cremation and his other affairs. When I arrived at the airport for my flight to London on the day I left Port Elizabeth for the last time, she was waiting outside the departure terminal to say goodbye. Linda-Louise was, and still is, one of those rare people who will always be a true friend, through the good and bad times.

As I boarded the plane, I felt a strange sense of liberation. Soon I would be an ordinary person, trying to live an ordinary and hopefully meaningful life, and not a 'marked' person who made people uncomfortable. I would never again have to see people I had known for many years dodge and dive to avoid me, or people scuttling past without much more than a quick "hi", desperate not to stop and chat. What had happened to our family would always be an integral part of our lives, and it would forever define me, but I hoped that in a new environment, surrounded by new people, I would just be accepted for myself.

CHAPTER 24

My flight arrived at Heathrow airport early on the morning of 22 February, and it was a novel experience for me to scan my newly acquired British passport for the first time, as I was waved through border control with a smile. What a change from the previous occasions when I had to wait for ages in a slow-moving queue, and then be questioned by border control officials who always seemed rather suspicious of incoming visitors.

Despite my fatigue after the busy three weeks in Port Elizabeth, and the long flight, I was very happy to be back with Catherine, and I was raring to go. We only had two weeks in which to pack everything and get ready for the removal van, and I knew we had a busy time ahead of us. Our biggest problem would be a lack of boxes, so once again, one of our daily jobs was to go from shop to shop, asking for empty boxes. We did this for a few days, but it became quite tedious, not to mention unpleasant in the cold, dark and wet weather, so we decided to buy a few boxes online. They were quite cheap, and I thought it would solve our problem, but when they arrived we found that they were much too large to fill with items such as books or crockery, because that would make them too heavy to move. The money spent was not wasted though, because they were perfect for duvets, blankets, pillows, towels and other linen, and we could wrap the more fragile things such as our flatscreen television, as well as other breakable items in the towels and pad them well with the duvets, which was very handy indeed. But we still needed lots of smaller boxes, so unfortunately we had no choice but to hit the road on foot again and ask around for empty boxes. I would never have thought that picking up a good stash of empty cardboard boxes would feel as if I had hit the jackpot and won a pot of gold, but it just goes to show that everything in life is relative, and one person's unwanted cardboard box will be another person's much needed cardboard box for packing.

All the plans were in place for our pets to make the long journey to Scotland, but there were still a few things that needed to be considered in advance of their arrival. Most importantly we needed to buy two large and spacious new parrot cages and have them delivered to our house in Cricklewood before we left, and we also wanted to stock up on new litterboxes and cat litter for the cats. With Move-a-Pet handling all the documentation of our pets, and with everything else concerning their relocation neatly falling into place, it seemed things were working out well. But then, why should things go smoothly, when they can go wrong?

Two days before Catherine and I were due to leave London for Arran, and just *one week* before Mia and the three cats were due to leave South Africa and embark on their long flight to Edinburgh, I received a message from our Move-a-Pet agent that Qatar Air had informed her they don't fly terriers. Mia weighed all of two kilograms, so the only risk she would pose is to kill someone with her cuteness. But Qatar Air were adamant that they do not fly terriers, which meant we now had exactly one week to deal with that unexpected crisis. It was a panicked scramble for our agent to find an airline, within the time frame we had to comply with, who could fly Mia and the cats to Edinburgh on 15 March. We didn't want them to fly on separate flights, because that would mean an extra trip from Arran to Edinburgh to fetch them. As it was, our planned trip to collect them would involve taking a bus to the ferry terminal in Brodick, the ferry from Brodick to Ardrossan Harbour on the mainland, collecting our rental car, and driving to Edinburgh to collect the cats and Mia. And afterwards we would have to return to Ardrossan Harbour and drop off the rental car, take the ferry back to Brodick on Arran, and then take a bus from Brodick to our house in Whiting Bay. We were already daunted by the very thought of doing it once with Mia and the cats in March, and then again with Percy and the parrots in April, and we certainly did not want to make a third trip to Edinburgh. It was an anxious few hours before we received the good news from our very capable agent at Move-a-Pet that she had managed to secure a booking for Mia and the cats on a Lufthansa flight, on their original departure date. The problem was solved, and the panic was over, but it didn't come cheap. It cost us handsomely to move the flight, although I will admit that by that stage we would have paid whatever was needed to get them on the same flight within the prescribed time frame. We were starting to run out of time, we were running out of steam, and we just wanted everything over and done with.

Meanwhile, Catherine and I were very busy packing up in Cricklewood. Hour after hour we kept filling what at times seemed to be endless boxes, duct taping them closed, and marking them clearly for easy identification in our new home. As the rooms emptied, the stacks of boxes got higher and higher, until finally, on the night of 8 March, everything was packed. All we had kept out were two stainless steel goblets for us to use as we sustained ourselves with some wine, two plastic bowls to eat out of and two spoons. We also had a few basic things such as toiletries and a change of clothes, and of course, the budgie food and all Ada's requirements for the next few days. But at last we were packed and ready, and the next step would be our journey to Arran.

At the end of our final and very busy day of packing, we took ourselves off to the local Wetherspoons for supper as a treat. We have always been great fans of Wetherspoons, no matter where in the UK, because we like the jovial and busy atmosphere, the food is reliably good for pub food and very reasonably priced, and they always have excellent choices of ales and beers on tap. Catherine and I settled down to a hot meal and a pint or two as we recharged our batteries, making our last-minute plans. The removal company would be arriving early the following morning, and once they were on their way, we would spend our last night in London.

We were both up and about very early the next morning, hastily packing the last few items, but we ran out of duct tape before we had sealed all the boxes, so Catherine had to make a last-minute dash to the corner shop in Edgeware Road to buy more duct tape. She returned just in time, minutes after the removal truck had pulled up outside our house at exactly eight o'clock on the dot. We were frantically taping the last few boxes closed as the two very competent and energetic removal men started carrying our boxes to the truck, with our furniture and boxes seemingly flying out of our house at breakneck speed. Despite having to load up in the rain, they did an excellent job, and soon the house was empty, the loaded removal truck was pulling away, and our furniture and household goods were on their way to Ardrossan, and then to Arran. It was an eerie feeling standing in the empty living room, with our voices echoing in the silence, with memories lurking in the corners and hanging in the air, and I couldn't help thinking of William who had spent his last few hours in that same room. There were happy memories too, but the overriding memory for me was one of sadness.

During the removal of our furniture and household goods Catherine had kept Ada upstairs in the bathroom, and as soon as the removal men had left she opened the door and let her out. At first Ada was quite bewildered to be in an empty house, creeping around very cautiously, but she soon perked up when we tossed a ping pong ball into the empty living room, and she pranced around after the ball with great energy. Meanwhile Catherine and I decided to make ourselves comfortable in her empty bedroom, and we settled ourselves down on the carpet. We had bought sandwiches from the Co-Op, and of course a bottle of wine, and we enjoyed a quiet evening in our deserted little house for the last night. After many long and difficult months we both had our own thoughts and emotions to deal with, but we felt focused and positive, and we were relieved that the time had finally arrived for us to make a new start on Arran.

With no furniture left in the house, Catherine was going to sleep on the floor of her bedroom, and our neighbours had kindly lent her pillows and blankets to keep her comfortable. I was going to spend the night at a small guesthouse not far from the house, because sleeping on the floor was not something I was very keen to do. I have more than enough issues with a bad back and aching bones. All I wanted to do on that last night was to take a hot shower, spend some time watching whatever was on the television to take my mind off everything, and then try and have a decent rest in a warm bed. As things turned out I was disappointed on all counts: There was no hot water, the television didn't work, the bed was as hard as a board, and there was only one thin blanket. Catherine was probably a lot more comfortable on the floor.

Since sleepless nights had become my new normal, I tossed and turned all night, thinking of all the possible things that could go wrong. One of my biggest concerns remained the risk that the ferry may be cancelled due to bad weather, leaving us in limbo with a cat and two budgies. It was a long night as I lay awake on the hard bed, trying to keep warm under the threadbare blanket, worrying about every unfortunate possibility my overactive imagination could come up with, and I was very happy to see the first light of day. I was up early because I couldn't wait to get going, and after dressing and gathering together the few belongings I had taken with me, I set off for our house, stopping at the Co-Op on my way to buy pre-packed sandwiches and fruit juice for our trip on the train. The count-down to the last leg of our journey had started and I was ready to face the day I had been working up to for six months, even if I had absolutely no idea what the day would bring. All I knew was that soon we would say goodbye to our little house in Cricklewood and leave London for the Isle of Arran.

CHAPTER 25

Our journey would involve taking a bus from Cricklewood to Euston Station, a train from Euston Station to Glasgow Central Station, and after sleeping over in Glasgow we would be taking a train from Glasgow to Ardrossan. From Ardrossan we would take the ferry to Brodick on the Isle of Arran, and finally we would take a bus from Brodick to Whiting Bay. That much I did know, but there was one detail I didn't know. Unfortunately I hadn't paid much attention to exactly *where* our house was in Whiting Bay when we had gone to measure up the rooms. All I knew was that it was on the main road which runs around the island, so that narrowed things down slightly. It didn't narrow things down much, just slightly, but hopefully that would be enough for me to find it. I was sure I would recognize our house when I saw it, even if we had to wander around for a while, although I was rather worried about it. Of course, I didn't share my doubts with Catherine because I was quite sure she would not appreciate my vagueness about where our house was, so I kept quiet, kept my fingers crossed, and tried to be optimistic that everything would work out one way or the other. Patrick had sent me a WhatsApp message with basic directions of where the bus stop was, so at least I had a reasonably good idea of where we had to get off the bus. But that was still a day away and I had enough to worry about in the present, so I kept my doubts and worries to myself.

It was a cool and dull morning on the 9th of March when we stepped out of our little house in Cricklewood for the last time, and I pulled the door closed behind me. Our luggage included a huge and heavy bright pink suitcase on wheels, two full backpacks, a laptop bag, a cat, two budgies, and Milosz the Madagascan Hissing Cockroach. Yes, Catherine had a pet cockroach.

Just before we left, I went through my checklist again:
Ada in cat carrier - check.
Budgies in travel cage - check.
Milosz the cockroach in his little travel box - check.
Cat food - check.
Cat bowls - check.
Budgie food - check.
Water - check.
Towels to cover cat and budgies - check.
Litter box - check.
Cat litter - check.
Suitcase, rucksacks and laptop bag packed - check.
Hotel booking at pet friendly place in Glasgow - check.
Sanity – questionable…….

After arriving at Euston Station we made our way to our platform, with me dragging the large suitcase and both of us heavily weighed down by our backpacks, the laptop bag, the cat carrier, and the budgie cage. The station was teeming with people, which did not make for a happy cat, and she let us know how she was feeling with worried little meows from under her cover. The situation did not improve when we hauled ourselves onto the train and found it was packed to capacity, with hardly space to turn. I couldn't find anywhere to put our large suitcase because all the luggage racks were full, so I had no choice but to shove it into a gap between two seats and hope it would stay there. The train hadn't even left the station yet and I was already exhausted. But I was very, very grateful that Patrick had booked seats for us with a table, because there was absolutely nowhere to put the cat carrier and the budgie cage. We were forced to put them on the table in front of us, right up against our faces to leave enough space on the table for anyone sitting opposite us, and as luck would have it a rather grumpy elderly couple sat down in those seats and immediately started complaining loudly. We pulled the cage and the cat carrier as close to our faces as possible, but they carried on mumbling and grumbling to each other, making sure we could hear their displeasure. Despite our efforts, we knew they would continue their complaining, so we just hid behind Ada and the budgies, and left them to wallow in their misery. The cat and the budgies were confined, what more could we do?

It was a long and tiresome train journey, with the cat and budgies in our faces and our backpacks and laptop bag at our feet, and every time the train entered a tunnel, the two budgies would set up an almighty chatter about what was going on, which did not endear us to the grumpy couple in any way whatsoever. Eventually Catherine and I agreed that we both needed a glass of wine to make our very cramped and awkward train journey a bit more agreeable, so I clambered over the luggage at my feet, and I made my way to the train canteen to buy two small bottles of red wine. With the cat and budgies in our faces, and the train rocking from side to side, it was somewhat of a challenge to pour the wine and to drink it without spilling, but we managed rather well and with each sip we cared less about the unpleasant couple, who by this time had fallen into quiet sulking. As for us, we kept a low profile and sipped our wine in peace, knowing that every minute was taking us closer to Glasgow, and to the end of our cramped journey.

To pass the time Catherine was reading TripAdvisor reviews about the hotel we had booked into for the night, and the more she read, the paler she got, until she resembled a paler shade of green.

"Mom, just listen to this", she said, and she went on to read several reviews to me. No wonder she looked a pale shade of green – the reviews were terrible, with extremely unsavoury comments about the bedding, and with some people even suggesting the place should be condemned.

"Well, we don't have anywhere else to go, so we will just have to bite the bullet and hope for the best", I told her. After all, some of the reviews were a few months old, and hopefully things had changed for the better.

She looked mortified, but she understood that we had no choice. Eventually we agreed that if the reviews were right and things were truly that bad, we would stay fully dressed and each sit in a chair all night, just allowing Ada to have the evening out of her cat carrier and access to her litter box, and then we would leave very early the next morning. I told Catherine to stop reading the reviews because there was a fifty-fifty chance that things were not that bad, but for the rest of the journey we both felt less than thrilled about the prospect of what we may have to deal with at the hotel.

After a very long day the train finally pulled in at Glasgow Central Station. We were tired and hungry, and I knew there was a Wetherspoons pub on the way to our hotel, although I wasn't sure about their pet policy. Ada was safely in a carrier and the budgies were in their cage, so they wouldn't bother anyone, but would we be allowed to take them in? We didn't know, but I decided that we were going to try our luck anyway. As we reached the pub I saw a table right at the entrance, and I said to Catherine we should just nip in and park the budgies and Ada under the table before anyone saw us, and then we had to hope they would all shut up. After all, the budgies had been chirping all day, and Ada had done her fair bit of complaining, so hopefully they were all tired out. Our luck held, because as we enjoyed our first hot meal in two days, and the pints of ale went down like liquid gold, everyone under the table stayed absolutely quiet. Not a single chirp or meow was heard from beneath the table.

We felt much stronger after the meal, and once we had regained our energy, and our courage, we set off for our hotel feeling rather cautious about what we would find there. Would it really be as dirty and as disgusting as the reviewers said on TripAdvisor? We were about to find out.

It was a small budget hotel, rather dingy, but not at all as bad as we thought it may be. The first thing Catherine spotted as we were checking in was a certificate from Health and Safety above the reception desk, and she nudged me to draw my attention to it. Clearly things had improved since the awful reviews on TripAdvisor, and that was rather encouraging to note. Our room was very basic with a threadbare carpet, but it was neat and clean, the bedding was clean, and the bathroom was spotless, even if the basin had a tenuous grip to the wall and the bath was old and stained. After the long train journey we were very tired, and a bed was all we needed. Sleep was another matter though, because Ada spent the first few hours prowling up and down, jumping on us, sniffing around, and just generally poking her face everywhere. Obviously spending a whole day in her cat carrier meant she now had plenty of energy to spare. We may have been hoping for some sleep, but she most certainly wasn't, and she was not about to let us nod off and leave her without company. After annoying us for several hours, she finally ran out of energy and snuggled in with Catherine for a short nap, and we managed to get about two hours' sleep, before we were up again to face the new day and our final stretch to Arran.

With Ada fed, watered, and back in her cat carrier for the next leg of our journey, we did a final check to see that we didn't leave anything behind, and then set off for Glasgow Station, looking and feeling like packhorses with all our luggage. The last part of our journey would involve a one-hour train trip to Ardrossan Harbour, a 55-minute ferry trip to Brodick, a 20-minute bus trip from Brodick to Whiting Bay, and then a short walk to the house. That is, if I managed to get us off at the correct bus stop, and if I managed to find our house without any difficulties.

We were back at the station very early, and after buying our train and ferry tickets we looked for a quiet place to wait with Ada and the budgies, who were all quite agitated by the loud noises of the station. Finding a quiet place in a hustling and bustling train station is as difficult as trying to find water in a parched well, but we eventually found a slightly less noisy corner close enough to our platform, where we kept our eyes on the notice board eagerly waiting to board the train. As soon as the notification went up that we could board we were first on the train, with our heavy suitcase, two backpacks, laptop bag, budgies and cat.

"We are getting there", I said to Catherine, as we sat back and waited for the train to leave.

A few minutes before the train was due to depart we heard the announcement of stations where our train was stopping. I wasn't paying much attention, but I noticed that Catherine was listening very intently, which was just as well.

"Mom, this train is not going to Ardrossan!" she said urgently.

"What do you mean?" I asked.

"This train is not going to Ardrossan. They just said so", she insisted.

I couldn't believe my ears! As luck would have it, the conductor was standing right outside our door, so I asked him if the train was going to Ardrossan.

"No, the train to Ardrossan was just in front of this one, and it left about ten minutes ago. This train is leaving soon", he replied.

We were on the wrong train. So much for me saying "we are getting there", when in reality we would not be "getting there" any time soon if we were on the wrong train.

I never thought it was possible to offload so much luggage in such a short time, but we got everything off just before the doors slammed closed and the train left. Fortunately it was not a complete disaster, because there was another train to Ardrossan about thirty minutes later, although it did mean we would miss the early ferry, which was the ferry the removal truck with our furniture was on. So, our day did not start off quite the way I had hoped.

We took the next train to Ardrossan, but when we arrived at the terminal we were very disappointed to learn that we would have a long wait for the next ferry. It wasn't the best news of the day, but at least the ferry terminal was quiet, so we found ourselves a convenient place to sit down and wait. The ferry terminal may have been quiet when we arrived, but unfortunately our day was about to get even more difficult when several young families arrived with their hordes of undisciplined offspring. It was bedlam as their brats started running around, jumping on the seats, shrieking loudly, chasing each other around as if they were in a play park. The term 'feral' came to mind. Meanwhile the parents ever so serenely ignored the chaos that their offspring were inflicting on the rest of us. Ada started getting very agitated by the shrieks and noise, so we moved as far away from them as we could, but to no avail, because they were soon in every corner and on every seat of the terminal waiting room. Eventually I ran out of tolerance and told a few of them very sternly to go away and not come close to us. It worked. But only for a few minutes. Soon they were back, chasing each other around, running on the seats and creating noise and havoc, knowing full well that their parents would allow them to do whatever they wished. Our nerves were stretched to breaking point by their noise, but mercifully, after what felt like a lifetime, the ferry came into view. We were the first in line to board, and I don't know where the parents and their brats went, but we never heard or saw them again. It was wishful thinking I know, but I had satisfying visions of them all locked in a soundproof cage. Parents and children together.

The ferry was packed and because we were seated in the pet owners' area, there were quite a few dogs yapping and barking. They were mostly well behaved, but Ada had never met any dogs before, so she was quite stressed. We were pretty stressed by that time as well, and we longed for a cool beer to wet our whistles, but we were seated right at the far end of the row, and we were completely boxed in by people and dogs, so we just had to stay put. At least we were on the ferry and our long journey from London to Arran was almost over. Because Catherine had never been to Arran before, she had admitted that she had no idea what she was letting herself in for, but she told us she would just take things as they came and try and get on with her life. As the island finally came into view I could barely believe that we had made it in one piece, and that my sanity was more or less still intact. The months leading up to that moment had been quite harrowing to say the least, and it was quite an emotional moment for me when I realised that we were about to disembark in Brodick, not as visitors, but as residents of the island.

As the ferry docked Catherine and I got ourselves, all our luggage, and the pets to the exit ahead of the other passengers to escape the rush, and as soon as the doors opened we were out, hauling everything down the gangway, and then to the bus terminal. We were a bit lost about which bus to take, but as we would discover very quickly, everyone on the island is very helpful and friendly and they will go the extra mile to help if they can. We were soon on the correct bus heading for Whiting Bay, and within minutes the two budgies Orfi and Jo started up an animated discussion about the new sounds and views, causing much laughter on the bus, which was a pleasant change after the grumpy couple on the train. Their cheerful chirping was the perfect icebreaker, and we were soon chatting to passengers around us, which eased our weary and stressed minds a bit. Of course, I still had my unmentioned concern about finding our house, and I kept my eyes on the road ahead. As we approached Whiting Bay the bus driver turned around briefly and asked where we wanted to be dropped off, and when I told him we needed to get off near Sandbraes Villa, but I wasn't sure where that was, he told me not to worry he would show us where to get off the bus, and where to find the house. He stopped the bus and pointed us in the right direction, towards the house, which was just a few yards away.

Dredging up my last shred of energy, I helped Catherine slowly pull and carry everything down the driveway of our new house. Our long and arduous journey was over, and we were home. By hook or by crook we had made it in one piece.

The previous owners were moving into a house up the road in the same village, and they had their own set of problems to deal with. Although they had been packed and ready to move in good time, the previous owner of their new home had not removed all his furniture from the house yet, so they couldn't move their furniture and household goods in. As we staggered down the driveway, they were frantically trying to clear enough space in their new house and trying to get the last few things out of our house. The removal van with our furniture and goods was parked up on the road waiting to unload, because they had to get the ferry back to the mainland, and I went and apologised about the delay, but they were not at all fazed. With wide smiles, they told me they were enjoying the experience of being on an island, coming on the ferry and having some time to admire the beautiful view across the sea to the mainland. I appreciated their optimism, but I was definitely feeling very edgy in case they missed the ferry because they were due on the last ferry of the day.

Fortunately we only had to wait for about an hour before the house was ready for us to move in, and they could bring their truck onto our driveway. Once again, they didn't waste a moment, as they unloaded the furniture and boxes at breakneck speed. At one point, and still smiling, they were confidently running from the truck to the house, carrying boxes which were marked 'fragile, contains glassware', without any apparent fear of dropping them at all. I felt far less confident about that, but I decided that the best thing to do was look the other way. Things were happening very quickly, and they seemed to know what they were doing, so the less I saw the better. Eventually they had all the boxes and goods off the truck, our beds assembled and the furniture in the right places, and we could wave them off as they left for Brodick in time for the ferry. They were a real delight as a team. Nothing was too much trouble for them, they worked fast and efficiently, and they never stopped smiling.

We had started our day in Glasgow by missing our train, we had navigated ourselves, the pets, and our luggage onto the ferry and then onto the bus, and we had overseen the unloading of our household goods. After a day which had started off with a rush of panic, everything was suddenly very quiet. Incredible, and unbelievably, the rush was over.

We didn't have much furniture because we had only brought our bed, a wardrobe and a dressing table for our bedroom, Catherine's bed, wardrobe and desk for her room, a few shelves, a table and four chairs, our sofa, the TV and a TV stand. And we had the little round garden table and chairs for the kitchen. We didn't have any curtains or rugs at all, and if we wanted our crockery, cutlery, books, bedding and linen, we would have to do some unpacking of boxes. We would get to the job of unpacking soon enough, but for the moment we just both wanted to take stock of our situation and gather our strength.

Catherine went to her side of the house to spend some time with Ada, who had been closed in a room away from the noise and action, because like us, she had also been through two long and stressful days, and she needed Catherine to spend quiet time with her to comfort and to reassure her. And on our side of the house, I wandered from silent room to silent room, trying to envisage how we would do things when our furniture and goods eventually arrived from South Africa, in late May. It still didn't feel like home, but I knew that as soon as I could put a few small and personal touches in place, that would change. In the earlier years of our marriage Patrick and I had moved around quite often because we lived in rental flats and every time the owners wanted to sell their flat, we would have to move. One year we moved three times, with three small boys in tow. But we had lived in our last home for almost three decades and it had become our comfort zone in every sense of the word. Now I was in a new home, and everything was unknown and different, and it was a lot smaller than what we were used to. It was going to take time for us to put our own personal stamp on our new home, but Patrick was due to arrive for a few days on 15 March, and I was hoping to have the house more or less comfortable and functional with the few things we had brought from London, before he arrived.

CHAPTER 26

With Ada fed and settled, we decided to head into the village in search of an eating establishment because we needed a hot meal and a good bottle of wine to perk us up and revive our flagging energy. Although we didn't know one end of the village from the other, we did know we had come in from the right side of our driveway and we hadn't seen many buildings on that side, so it made sense to turn left as we left our driveway and see what we could find. After walking for about twenty minutes, we reached a hardware store which also had a liquor license, and they sold a good choice of wines, so that was our first success of the evening. At least we had a bottle of red wine to fortify us - all we needed was a place to eat. A short distance after the hardware store we saw a small shop, with the proprietor standing outside the door. I asked her if there was anywhere close by for us to get a meal, and she replied, "Well this is your lucky day, just keep walking another ten minutes or so and you will see Felicity's. They serve a fish and chips special on Fridays, which is very tasty". My weary bones picked up the pace after hearing that. Having somewhere quiet to sit down, have a good meal and enjoy a glass or two of wine was going to be a sheer luxury. It felt as if we had left our little house in Cricklewood months ago, not just two days ago, but thankfully our journey had been far less stressful than I had feared it would be, and we hadn't encountered any serious problems. Inconveniences, yes. But serious problems, no.

The uncomfortable situation of the grumpy couple opposite us from London to Glasgow, the inconvenience of us missing our train to Ardrossan, and the awful brats at the ferry terminal were all forgotten as we tucked into the most delicious meal of fish and chips. The batter on the fish was crispy and golden, and the chips were perfect. The wine went down very well too, and gradually we could both feel our nerves unwind. After a rest and a hearty meal, we set off back to our house, ready to spend a few hours making our new home livable. Catherine went to her side of the house to do whatever unpacking she could do, and I started unpacking in our bedroom. For me, the first thing to do in a new home is to make the bed. Having the bed made up with familiar bedding seems to signal ownership of a bedroom, and it is also a comfort to know there is somewhere to sleep when one's energy finally runs out. With the bed made up and ready, I unpacked a few basic toiletries into the bathroom, I unpacked a few essentials such as the kettle, some mugs, plates and cutlery in the kitchen, and then I went to see how Catherine was doing. She had her own method of creating her new living space, which appeared to be rather haphazard to me, but she assured me that she had a plan on how to go about unpacking her things. For starters, she had connected up her computer, and she had music blaring to keep her going, and amidst the controlled and happy chaos, with Ada nosing around everywhere, the two of them were clearly doing just fine in their new territory. I said goodnight and left them to get on with it. The journey had well and truly caught up with me and I wanted to get to bed.

The next morning I woke very early, too restless to relax. The entire experience of the past few months, where everything had happened so fast, still hadn't quite sunk in completely. Looking through the window of what was to be our new study, I saw the dappled sunshine shining on a mass of yellow daffodils, as far as the eye could see. It was quite a surreal yet magical feeling to know that this was my new home, and despite the rather dull light of the early morning, I took a photograph of the daffodils through the window to capture the moment. Afterwards, when I checked the photo, I saw three very bright and perfectly clear orbs in the picture. Some people believe that orbs are angels or spirits of loved ones' manifesting, and although I don't have a strong view on that either way, I definitely have an open mind on all possibilities. All I know is that I have subsequently taken many photos from several different angles and at different times of the day, but I have never captured orbs in any of my photos again.

CHAPTER 27

Within two days of our arrival we had our first crisis. The little budgies had settled in immediately, but on the morning of our second day we noticed that Jo looked rather poorly. Birds often don't show they are ill until it is almost too late, so it is very important to act quickly when a bird appears unwell. We knew we had to get Jo to the vet as soon as possible, but it was a Sunday, which meant the vet was closed. And we didn't have a car. To complicate matters, we also had extremely poor mobile phone reception in our area, and it was only after several attempts that I finally managed to get through to the emergency number of the vets. Struggling with the poor reception, I explained our predicament to him, and he agreed to meet us at the vet surgery, but when he asked at what time he should meet us at there, I told him we were coming on a bus, and it would depend on what time the bus was coming through our village. Since we had only been in Whiting Bay for two days I didn't have the bus schedule yet. The vet then suggested that I phone him when we were on the bus, which we both agreed would be the best way to do things under the circumstances.

We had Jo's travelling cage inside a large carrier bag with a blanket over it to keep him warm and dry as we set off for Brodick on the bus, and for most of the way, I kept trying to phone the vet to let him know we were on our way, but the reception was so poor it was only as we approached Brodick that the phone reception was strong enough for me to connect with the vet. The vet surgery was quite a distance from the bus terminal, and it was only much later, when we knew our way around Brodick, that we realised there was a bus stop much closer. But at that time we only knew about the bus stance at the terminal, so there we were, walking much further than we needed to, in the wind and the rain with an ill budgie.

After a thorough examination, and the diagnosis of an infection, we left the vet surgery with medication for poor little Jo and made our way back to the terminal in the wind and the rain, only to discover that the next bus was two hours later, at 7pm! We simply could not sit in a bus shelter for two hours with a sick budgie, but the problem for us was that after only being there for two days, we had no idea of taxi services. Fortunately I managed to get the number of a taxi inside the ferry ticketing office and, struggling with a bad reception once again, I eventually contacted a taxi driver who arrived after about fifteen minutes. With that unexpected crisis hopefully dealt with, we spent the rest of the evening, and the following days, unpacking the boxes and slowly turning our new house into a relatively cozy home. It was still rather cold and stark without rugs and curtains, but at least we had the television and a sofa to sit on in the lounge, and we soon started to feel very comfortable in our semi-furnished house.

Five days after Catherine and I moved into our new house Patrick finally arrived for a short ten-day visit. The non-stop stress and strain of getting everything done was starting to take a toll on him, and he looked very tired, but we both knew that the end of our massive relocation was in sight, and we just needed to keep up the momentum and stay on course. Unfortunately there was no time for Patrick to rest after his arrival because we had to collect our Yorkie and our three cats from the Animal Reception Centre in Edinburgh the following day. They were due to land at 11.40 am, with an expected clearance time of approximately three hours, and we didn't want them to spend one minute longer in confinement than absolutely necessary, so we were eager to get there in good time. It wasn't going to be a simple exercise though because we didn't have a car yet, so we would be taking the early bus to the Brodick ferry terminal to get the first ferry of the day to Ardrossan, where we had to collect a rental car, and then we would have to make our way to the Animal Reception Centre outside Edinburgh airport. With a great deal of luck my navigation skills would hopefully get us there without any mishaps along the way, and we were hoping to arrive before the pets were ready for collection. Of course that was only one half of what we had to do, because after collecting the pets we had to get back to Ardrossan in time for the 6pm ferry. The timing would be rather tight, and it would very much depend on us finding our way there and back without wasting time by getting lost.

As we set off on the early bus to get the ferry we were both very much on edge. Our first big worry was how we would find the Animal Reception Centre because the map was not very detailed, and our second worry was getting back to Ardrossan in time for the ferry. The route there and back was completely unknown to us, and naturally we made it our business to worry about every single potential mishap we could think of, from beginning to end. But everything went surprisingly well. Our car was ready and waiting for us in Ardrossan, we made no wrong turns at all, and we arrived at the Centre in good time to collect Mia the Yorkie, Amadeus our Bluepoint Siamese, Raven our calico girl, and Victoria our black and white girl. Move-a-Pet had kept me updated on their progress across the miles, sending text messages when they departed from Port Elizabeth, when they landed at Johannesburg Airport and when they departed again, and the same when they landed in Frankfurt, and then when they left Frankfurt for Edinburgh. Knowing where they were was very helpful, but we were still anxious about how they would cope with such a long flight. As soon as we arrived, we went into the Reception Centre to find out the latest update on their flight and we were overjoyed to hear they had landed safely, and that they would be ready for collection as soon as the documentation had been checked.

After waiting in anticipation and with some anxiety a door finally opened and four pet travelling crates were carried through, although little Mia was not in her crate, she was being cradled in the arms of a young woman who was comforting her. Our three cats were each in their own crates and we could see three very anxious little faces peering out at us, but they were all safe and sound, and we were thrilled and relieved to have them with us again. We didn't have much time to waste though because we had to get back to Ardrossan in time for the ferry, so with help from the staff we loaded the three cat crates in the car, and with Mia on my lap, we set off on our return trip to Ardrossan, and then to Arran. The cats were very upset about the whole affair, and they kept up a steady chorus of cat complaints, with Patrick and I trying to calm them along the way. It didn't appease them one bit, and their endless caterwauling was so distracting that we got lost several times on the way back to Ardrossan. Our nerves were already rather frayed, and getting lost didn't help in any way whatsoever, but fortunately our mistakes did not cost us too much time and we made it to Ardrossan quite a while before the ferry was due to leave.

Once we were safely at Ardrossan Harbour I suggested to Patrick that we put all three cats into one crate because I thought that would make carrying them easier. At least we would only have to worry about being careful with one crate, while the other two could be hauled around in whichever way we had to. I also thought it would be comforting for them to be together in the same crate, and it did help them, because as soon as they were all together they settled down and complained less. We were rather worried about how we would deal with all the crates and with Mia, but we needn't have worried because we had many willing hands to help us up the gangway and onto the ferry. We sank into our seats feeling tired but absolutely exhilarated at the same time. This was the second last 'animal transport' we would have to make on the ferry, and it felt great to know that we were well and truly getting closer to the end of what had been an unbelievable, and almost impossible, decision just a few months earlier.

As soon as we were on our way Patrick went to the bar and ordered a well-deserved double whisky for himself and a glass of red wine for me, and we toasted our successful trip to Edinburgh and back. One more box was ticked, and we had one less worry to keep us awake at night. We still had quite a long way to go, but the list was getting shorter by the day, and we knew the end of our long and stressful move was slowly but surely coming closer.

When we berthed in Brodick we were overwhelmed by the kindness and willingness of people offering to help us with the four crates, first down the gangway of the ferry, and then to the waiting bus. We gratefully accepted all offers of help, and in double quick time we were on the bus, and on our way home. As the bus wound its way around the bends in the road from Brodick to Whiting Bay, it took me back to when Catherine and I had arrived just one week earlier, and we hadn't even moved into our house yet. It certainly didn't feel as if only one week had passed since the two of us had arrived in Whiting Bay, it felt as if we had been here for much longer.

When we reached the bus stop where we had to get off the bus, we were pleasantly surprised as the bus driver drove past the stop and pulled up right in front of our driveway to get us closer to home. He turned the bus off, and with another passenger, he helped us offload the crates into our driveway. Coming from a city, we thought it was exceptionally kind of the bus driver and those who were so keen to help us, but we soon learned that this attitude of kindness and willingness to help is not at all unusual on the island. Instead of being the exception, it is the norm.

CHAPTER 28

While we were preparing supper in the kitchen later that evening, our cats spent their time cautiously exploring their new home, creeping around on their bellies and sniffing every surface, with large anxious eyes. They kept coming back to see where we were, so we tried to keep everything calm and reassuring for them, but they were clearly very nervous and confused. Mia wasn't particularly stressed because she was usually in someone's arms or on a lap anyway, and that was where she spent her first evening with us after her long journey. We were in bed quite soon after supper, with Mia snuggled into her usual spot, between us on our bed. Victoria went to sleep on the sofa in the lounge, near a heater, and Raven took up her vigil on my chest. She did leave every so often, but only to return and sit on my chest again, as if to say: 'I am watching you. Don't go away'. Amadeus, being a Siamese cat, decided to tell me all about his experiences in great detail. Throughout the night, he kept coming to me and waking me with his loud voice and his paw on my face, complaining about what he had been through and what he thought of this strange new place, which, by the sound of his voice, wasn't much at all. Sleep was rather a disrupted affair, until he was finally satisfied that he had said everything that was worth saying, and just after five o'clock in the morning he crept under the duvet with me for a nap. A Siamese cat has only one voice volume, and that is loud, but I had missed him and his loud voice, and I had missed his little body snuggling up with me under the duvet.

It was good to have them with us, even if it meant I had Raven sitting on my chest all night, watching me like a hawk, and Amadeus complaining loudly into my ears.

On their first day in our house the cats spent most of the time tightly curled up together. They were still very stressed by everything, and they were clearly also feeling cold because they had left the very warm South African weather behind them and arrived in a rather cold Scotland. And for the moment, they knew nothing about the other cat on the opposite side of the house, behind a closed door, who would eventually join them, just as Ada was blissfully unaware of the small dog and three cats who had arrived, and of the large dog who was due to arrive later.

As lovely as it was to have Patrick with us, he had to return to Port Elizabeth after ten days, and once again we had to say goodbye to each other. But at least we were on our very last lap, and if everything went according to plan, he would finally be back with us within a month. In the space of that month he would have to tie up all the numerous loose ends at work and at home, oversee the sale of any furniture and household goods we were not bringing to Arran, and then deal with the three full days it would take the removal company to pack up our possessions. Thank goodness for WhatsApp, because we kept in touch throughout the entire process, and Patrick sent me dozens of photos every day, with three simple words: "Keep or sell?" This went on day after day, as he worked his way through our things, and at times we had to make really difficult choices. Many things which were still precious to us quite simply had to be sold, because our new house was so much smaller than our house in Port Elizabeth. It was only the knowledge that we had a new beginning on Arran to look forward to that kept us going. Meanwhile, all the documents required for Patrick's spousal visa had been submitted by the agent, and we were anxiously waiting and hoping to hear that the application had been successful.

Our three cats were still quite nervous in their new home, and matters were not improved at all by the arrival of Tiger, a local ginger cat who loves to visit different homes in our village. He used to spend a lot of time with the previous owners of our house, and Patrick and I had met Tiger when we came to Arran to measure the rooms of our house in January. At the time I had expressed my concerns to Patrick about the possible problems Tiger might cause with our own cats, because I could see that he was very much at home in what was soon to be our house. And as things turned out, it didn't take very long for the problem to rear its head. One morning, a few days after Patrick had left, an ear-piercing wail cut through the air. Victoria, our little black and white cat, was screaming loudly at a very bewildered ginger cat, who was sitting on the windowsill outside the utility room. Poor Tiger looked really upset. After all, he was just visiting the house where he had always been welcome, and he didn't understand what was happening. Within minutes our other two cats were at the window too, all fluffed up and shrieking like banshees. After getting the three little wild furies into our bedroom, I went around the house sticking newspaper over all the windows to block their view of a visiting ginger cat, and for the moment the drama was postponed. But we clearly had a problem on our hands because our garden was a part of Tiger's territory, and he was not about to stop coming around to our house or garden. Our cats had not even met Ada yet, and having an outsider cat upsetting them would only make things more unsettled and difficult. For the moment though, the windows had newspapers plastered across the lower sections to block the view of a poor confused Tiger, and an uneasy peace was temporarily restored. He still came around to see what was happening at our house, but he couldn't come in, and our cats couldn't see him because I had blocked all the views to the outside with newspapers. It certainly didn't deter Tiger though. He was very curious about the new felines in what he saw as his house, and he came around every day to see if I would let him in. Unfortunately for him that was out of the question, although it did leave me feeling very guilty about his new situation.

Because Mia is so tiny, and she is used to cats, we decided that she would be the first one to meet Ada. Holding her in my arms I showed her to Ada, and after a few hisses and growls from a suspicious cat, we thought that would be good enough for a first meeting. We repeated the cautious introduction for a few days, and Ada soon felt comfortable enough at the sight of Mia, but only if she remained in my arms. That was a good enough stage to reach, and not long after that we decided to introduce our cats, one at a time. We started with Victoria because she is usually a very easy-going cat, despite her venting such fury at the sight of Tiger. We allowed her and Ada to meet in a neutral part of the house and she made no fuss at all, she just sniffed the air as if to say, 'Well, this is interesting'. And then she ignored Ada. One cat down and two more to go. The next day we introduced Amadeus, and he too was totally unfazed. He was not interested in Ada at all, and after looking her over, he wandered off.

We could hardly believe how well the introductions were going, but we knew we still had Raven to contend with. She was going to be a whole different ballgame, and we didn't expect her to accept a new cat in her life without a fuss. She had a quirky and sneaky personality, and we knew she would be far less predictable. At first, she pretended she did not even notice Ada, but she was only biding her time. We stayed as vigilant as possible, but every time we let our guard down even a little bit, she would rush up to Ada and deliver a rapid smack. As we expected, she was not going to accept a new cat without trying to show that she was the boss cat. At least our living arrangements meant we could keep them separate very easily, and when we did bring them into each other's company, it involved plenty of catnip! It took us about three weeks to successfully introduce them all to Ada, with a good few cheeky spats from Raven, and it was only after I used a well-aimed spray bottle to get the message through to Raven that she was not going to get away with smacking Ada that she settled down and accepted the situation. Fortunately it was only necessary to use the spray bottle twice, although we still had to keep an eye on her because she would pretend to be completely disinterested in Ada, and then she would try her luck when she thought we were not watching her. It took time and patience, and a lot of cat treats and catnip, but eventually they all learned to live together in reasonable peace and harmony.

Meanwhile, Patrick was still in South Africa finalising many details and keeping in daily contact with updates. But his long and seemingly endless list was starting to get shorter, and the day for him to finally join us on Arran was getting closer.

Not long after we moved into our house Catherine decided to look for a job because she was anxious to start earning an income. The hospitality business on Arran is always looking for staff and she was quite happy to try her hand in a kitchen, in whichever situation was available. When she saw that a kitchen porter post was advertised for a restaurant in Blackwaterfoot, which is on the other side of the island, Catherine still felt it would be worth going for an interview to get started in some form of employment. But during the interview it soon became clear that working in Blackwaterfoot would not be practical. The bus from

Whiting Bay to Blackwaterfoot takes almost an hour on the narrow winding road, and since the shifts started in the late afternoon, and there was no bus service back to Whiting Bay in the evenings, it was completely out of the question for her to take up the job. She was rather disappointed, but I assured her that it was still early days, and that there would no doubt be a more suitable kitchen porter position sooner or later. As things turned out, she didn't have long to wait, because barely a week later she saw a post advertising the position of a kitchen porter on a local Facebook page, and the restaurant was in Brodick, which has a regular bus service to and from Whiting Bay. She immediately sent them a request saying she was interested in applying for the position, and the response arrived a few minutes later: "Come in for a wee chat in the morning, and you can have a trial shift".

She arranged to meet with them at ten o'clock the next morning for the interview and to work a trial shift, and we were at the bus stop in good time, although we stood inside the bus shelter to keep out of the biting wind. We were still waiting in the bus shelter when we heard the bus rumble past us. The bus driver hadn't seen us, and we were stranded until the next bus, which would only be passing through an hour later! Naturally Catherine didn't want to be late for her appointment, but she had no mobile reception to phone and let them know about her predicament. It certainly wasn't a good start if she was hoping to get the job, so I reckoned that a desperate situation called for desperate measures, and I decided to disregard my late Mother's advice when I was young, about never, ever hitchhiking. I told Catherine to stand by because I was going to start thumbing a lift. I don't think she ever expected to see her mother thumbing a lift next to a road, but this was island life, and I was prepared to try a different way of doing things, especially since we were in something of a pickle. One car after the other whizzed past, and I was starting to feel quite desperate, but eventually a very friendly man stopped and offered us a lift. He was only going as far as Lamlash, which is more or less halfway, but we gratefully accepted his offer of a lift, and after he dropped us off in Lamlash my thumb was only out for about five minutes or so when a lady pulled over and offered us a lift to Brodick. Despite our unexpected way of getting there, Catherine was only ten minutes late for the appointment, and she had a job.

CHAPTER 29

After many long months of planning, panicking, dealing with setbacks, suffering sleepless nights and anxious days, the moment finally arrived for Patrick to join us on Arran. To our great relief his visa had been granted, and the countdown to his departure started. It had been a trying time for him in Port Elizabeth, overseeing the sale of many of our things that meant a lot to him, supervising the packing of our remaining goods into the huge removal truck, and finally the very difficult day when he had to say goodbye to our two old dogs, Roxie and Shadow, and let our vet send them on their final journey. They were both too old and too frail to make the long flight to Scotland, and in truth, they had both been living on borrowed time for quite a while. On their last night Patrick had made a barbecue especially for them, something they both loved, and he had given them their goodbye feast. Our wonderful vet would come to the house the following morning to spare them the unnecessary stress of going to his surgery.

And then, at last, the day dawned for him to say goodbye to our old family home and set off on his journey to Arran, just as I had done two months earlier. Percy and our two parrots, Paulie and Riley, who were booked on the same flight as Patrick, were to be collected at 3.30 am on the morning of 20 April, because they had to be given the all-clear by the State Vet, before being dropped off at Port Elizabeth airport by 6 am. Despite his fatigue, Patrick had to be up at about 3 am to get Percy and the parrots into their travelling crates before Move-a-Pet arrived to pick them up. After they left he was completely alone in the empty house, until our dear friend Linda-Louise arrived to take him to Port Elizabeth Airport. It was almost impossible to believe that Patrick would soon be on his way to us, and that all our months of stress were almost over. I was going to meet him at Edinburgh Airport and had booked a hotel room near Edinburgh Zoo. It was our final big hurdle, and now that we were close to the end of our difficult journey, I think it would be safe to say that we were both hanging on to our courage and focus by our fingertips. But everything went well, and Patrick's flight landed at Edinburgh airport right on time, on the morning of 21 April 2017. In a movie there would probably have been some cheesy background music and a slow-motion reunion in the arrival hall of the airport. In reality, we just embraced in silence and gratitude, and perhaps even in some disbelief, that we were finally together again, after having climbed the proverbial mountain we had set off to conquer in September, a mere seven months earlier.

Percy, Riley and Paulie would be at the Animal Reception Centre after their long flight, just as Mia and the three cats had been one month earlier, and we were very keen to get there and find out when they would be ready for collection after their documents were processed. We picked up the rental car and made our way to the Reception Centre, very much hoping to hear that we wouldn't have to wait for more than about three hours. Our trip was going to involve driving from Edinburgh to Prestwick Airport to drop off the rental car, and then we had to get a taxi from there to Ardrossan Harbour. We were really hoping to be in Ardrossan in good time for the early afternoon ferry back to Arran, but our hopes were dashed when we were told that the State Vet would only be coming in at 9.30 am, and that it would take about five hours to get clearance for the parrots. As I had discovered when arranging the relocation of Riley and Paulie from South Africa to the UK, taking parrots, and particularly an African Grey, across international borders is complicated and there are very strict requirements. It involves endless documentation and certification, which upon arrival first needs to be emailed to Manchester for CITES clearance, and then it gets emailed back to the Animal Clearance Centre, where some poor soul has to get into a car and drive to customs at the Edinburgh Airport to have all the papers checked and approved. As the hours ticked by, our hopes of catching an earlier ferry faded, and we were forced to readjust our plans, so we started hoping that at least we would make the 6pm ferry. The last ferry to the Isle of Arran would be at 8.30pm, and after the fifty-five-minute crossing and twenty-minute bus trip, it would mean we would only arrive home when it was almost 10pm. Patrick was well and truly exhausted, and Percy and the parrots had been through a traumatic experience, so we were very anxious to get home as soon as we could. But there was nothing we could do other than wait, so we went to a local hotel and had lunch, constantly checking our phones for a message from the Animal Reception Centre, and feeling more and more anxious every time we checked and there was no message. By the time we were finally allowed to collect Percy and the parrots, it was 3pm. That gave us less than three hours to get to Prestwick airport if everything went to plan and we didn't get lost along the way. After dropping the car off at the airport we had to contact a taxi driver to get us to Ardrossan before the 6pm ferry departed. To make things even more difficult, we didn't have a road map or Satnav to help us stay on the right highway, so we would need all the luck we could get.

Fortunately for us, Lady Luck was on our side because we managed to stay on the right highway and find Prestwick airport without getting lost. So far so good. But things were starting to go awry for us, because by the time we arrived at Prestwick Airport it was already 5pm. We were still desperately hoping to get the 6pm ferry, but passengers are supposed to board at least ten minutes before the ferry sails, which meant that effectively we had fifty minutes to get from Prestwick airport to Ardrossan. We would clearly need a lot more than luck; we would need a miracle. With precious minutes ticking by, we struggled at first to find the car rental office, which had no signage at all, but when we did finally locate the office we had the good fortune of dealing with a delightful man who phoned a taxi for us. Unfortunately things were complicated by the fact that it was the Scottish Grand National, and taxis were very busy, which meant the taxi only arrived at 5.30pm. Our hopes of catching the 6pm ferry were seriously fading, and they were almost completely dashed when the taxi driver said it usually took about forty minutes to Ardrossan.

The very thought of spending another three hours waiting with the pets was almost too much to bear, and we both pinned our hopes on the off chance that we would get to Ardrossan in time for the ferry. It was unlikely, but we were hoping! The taxi driver calmly set off, promising us that although he would stick to the speed limit, he would do his best to get us to Ardrossan in time for the ferry, and meanwhile he kept up light-hearted banter all the way, informing us that we were very lucky it was the Scottish Grand National, because that meant the roads were very quiet. We were still hanging onto a thread of optimism, but we were slowly starting to think we were going to miss the ferry after all.

As we finally approached Ardrossan Harbour we saw that the ferry was still there, and without even thinking, and after a hasty, "Thank you so much!" to the taxi driver, I jumped out of the still moving vehicle with Percy on his lead, and I ran ahead to buy our ferry tickets, while Patrick hastily paid the taxi driver and gathered the parrot crates and his luggage. With our ferry tickets in hand, a heavy backpack bouncing up and down on my back, and dragging a suitcase behind me, Percy and I hurtled up the gangplank, with Patrick hot on my heels, hauling his huge suitcase and two parrot crates up the gangplank with some help from ferry staff. We were the last to board as we squeaked in at the very last minute, and the gates closed behind us.

To say we were completely knackered would be an understatement, and as we sank into our seats and tried to gather our wits, we could barely believe we had made it. It had taken a hefty helping of luck and good fortune, but we were on the 6pm ferry, and on our way back to Arran. After many months of anguish and long separations, we would soon be home and dry, and most importantly, we would be together again.

Percy is an African Dog, also known as Canis Africanus, or as these dogs are called in some circles in South Africa, a 'street mix', and he received quite a lot of attention from our fellow passengers, with everyone wanting to know what breed he was. By this time he was so tired that he just allowed everyone to pet him and fuss over him. He even ignored all the other dogs, despite not being keen on other dogs at all. The parrots also caused quite a stir because it is not often that two parrots travel on the ferry to Arran, and our trip across the Clyde from Ardrossan to Brodick passed very quickly as we were inundated by questions from the curious passengers. Our last lap was the bus trip from the Brodick ferry terminal to Whiting Bay, where the budgies had caused some interest on the bus a month earlier, and once again there was a great deal of curiosity about Percy and the two parrots. Percy was almost asleep on his legs he was so exhausted, but Paulie the parrot was very vocal, causing some hilarity with her wolf whistling and "hello Paulie" comments to anyone who would listen. Just as on the ferry, the bus trip went very quickly, and when we reached Whiting Bay the bus driver once again was extremely friendly and helpful. He took us to our gate instead of to the bus stop a few meters down the road, and he and a few other passengers helped us offload the bird crates and Patrick's luggage. It was incredible, but we had managed to successfully pull off our epic move, and at long last we were home.

The many weeks and months of stress took a toll on Patrick, and not long after his arrival he started to feel very unwell with relentless pains in his stomach. His body was clearly telling him that it had been pushed to the limit. The best thing for him was to rest as much as possible, as I plied him with cups of chamomile tea to ease the cramps, while he rested on the bed. At least we had time to rest and gather our strength for a few weeks, while we waited for the huge container with our worldly goods to arrive from South Africa, and there was no reason why, after several months of stress, he should not just go with the flow and allow himself time to unwind and de-stress until he felt better again.

Our furniture and household goods were due to arrive at the end of May, and although we were quite comfortable, we were all looking forward to the day when we would be reunited with our things from South Africa, and we could finally make our new home the way we wanted it to be. It was going to be quite a job to unpack, unwrap and get everything in the right place. And by the right place I mean exactly where we had decided things would fit, and where every item would have to go. Patrick had measured each room, and we had measured the furniture, to make sure we had space for the things we were bringing with us, but there would not be a corner to spare.

Trying to figure out where we would hang our many artworks and framed photos was more of a challenge. Our house in Port Elizabeth was very large, and the passage was wide enough to form a gallery for our collection of family photos. The house had been the British Consulate many years before we bought it, and it was very spacious with large reception rooms, and obviously a lot of wall space for art works and pictures. Our new house didn't have a great deal of wall space at all, and we knew it was going to be a challenge finding space not only for our artworks, but also for our family photos, of which some dated back to the early 1900's.

Our very first large project was to have an enclosed cat garden constructed. Our cats are not allowed to roam, and we needed to have something built to provide a safe garden space for them. Nobody locks their doors on the island, and it is not at all unusual for neighbours to open a door to drop something off in your absence. The Posties on the island are also used to delivering the mail by just opening the gates, or the front doors, and putting the mail or parcels inside. After living in constant fear of being attacked in South Africa due to the high crime rate, this was very new to us. It was wonderful to have that level of trust around us, but the snag was that people may leave the gate or door open, allowing our cats to get out and into the road. After looking at different options we decided to have a very high palisade fence put up, with gates that can be locked from the inside or outside, and catproof fencing on the inside of the palisade fence. Some months later we heard that the villagers around us were most perplexed by the high fence, and many tongues were wagging about the strange actions of the new inhabitants in the village. Crime is almost non-existent here, and they couldn't understand who we wanted to keep out. It took us quite a while to get the word out around the village that we didn't want to keep anyone out, we wanted to keep our cats in.

CHAPTER 30

One month after Patrick's arrival the happy day finally dawned for the arrival of our furniture and household goods. It took careful maneuvering by the truck driver to get the huge truck down our driveway, and to park it in a rather small area, but he didn't seem too fazed by the tight squeeze. He was obviously used to handling such a massive vehicle, and it seemed that we were far more worried about it than the driver was.

With the truck parked, the removal men started off-loading our furniture and, under our direction, they carried everything into the house and placed things in the correct rooms. After the furniture came the boxes. They just kept coming, until we had boxes stacked three high on the table in the conservatory, boxes underneath the table, and boxes stacked four or five high in the spare bedroom and downstairs bathroom. I stopped counting at box number 334, because there were many more to come, but eventually the last box was carried in, everything was delivered, and we waved the removal men off as they left to get the ferry back to the mainland.

The furniture was pretty much in the correct place, but we still had all the boxes to unpack. There were so many that we couldn't afford to be fussy about what we unpacked first, although the one box we were rather keen to find was the box of curtains, especially for the bedrooms. It was like winning the lottery when Patrick found it within a few days, and at last we had curtains, which made a huge difference, especially because the sun was starting to rise very early by then. We tried to unpack as much as possible every day, and slowly but surely our house became a comfortable home as rugs went down, pictures and artworks went up, and all the creature comforts we were able to bring with us started to fill the rooms.

Not long after Patrick's arrival we started to discuss what we should do with William's ashes. Scattering them in the sea was an option, but we favoured the idea of burying his ashes in our garden. We have a large garden, with many trees as well as the burn, or stream, which runs through the property, so there were several really beautiful places where we could lay his ashes to rest. One day I was strolling around trying to find the best place and I spotted a large grey feather lying between two trees next to the burn. I immediately thought the feather was a helpful sign, because it is a very tranquil and beautiful place, with the tinkling sounds of the burn in the background, and birdsong in the trees. It is as beautiful as the forest clearing, next to the river, where we laid Alex's ashes to rest in 2009.

After burying William's ashes, Patrick, Catherine and I all took turns building a stone cairn for him. We kept it simple, with no markers of any kind, because we just wanted to mark his resting place for ourselves, without anything more. There is no marker to show where Alex is buried either, only the tree we planted. The owners of the wine farm wisely felt that because he was well known in music circles, and his death had been widely publicised at the time, any marker with his name on would potentially bring too much attention to his burial place. The tree would be his marker and there was no need to put his name anywhere. For William, the stone cairn would be his marker.

The first person to come and visit us on the island was Nadiah, a friend of Alex's. She had briefly met Alex in 2007, at the Genting International Jazz Festival in Malaysia, and like so many other people, she had contacted me after he died. We kept in touch afterwards and when she came to visit us in May 2017, even before our furniture arrived from South Africa, we decided that it would be a good time to build a small memorial cairn for Alex while she was with us. We didn't have any fixed ideas of where to build it or what to build, but we went down to the beach for a walk and while we were there, we all looked out for a few flat stones which may be suitable for building a small cairn. As we were walking along the beach a little robin appeared out of nowhere, and it perched on a rock just ahead of us, keeping tiny beady eyes on us. It caught our attention because every time we paused the robin would perch on a rock, waiting and watching, until we moved again, and then it would fly ahead, perch on a rock, and wait for us to catch up. It seemed as if the little bird was communicating with us in some way, and the interesting thing is we had never seen a robin on the beach before, and we have never seen a robin on beach again since that day. It was quite extraordinary.

Back at our house we settled on a secluded place under a tree, next to the burn, to build a small memorial cairn for Alex. It was just a few yards away from William's burial cairn, and the only adornments on both cairns are a few seashells and a large scallop shell on each.

CHAPTER 31

When we made the decision to pack up our worldly goods and move to a small Scottish island, leaving everything we knew behind us, we had no idea whatsoever how we were going to earn a living. We quite simply put it out of our minds because we had enough to worry about, and we decided to cross that bridge when we absolutely had to. Of course, we knew our lifestyle would have to change to fit in with our new financial situation, and we also realised that for the first time in many years we would be living on a limited budget. Patrick was giving up a very successful and lucrative practice as an advocate in South Africa, and we would have to adapt to our changed circumstances. We were planning to eventually buy and run a holiday flat as a form of income, but we would first have to find a suitable flat before that plan could be put into motion. Other than that, we didn't have any definite ideas on earning an income. Our lifestyle of travelling, entertaining, going to shows and dining in restaurants would radically change, but becoming homebirds was not something that worried us at all. After a very dark and difficult year it suited us perfectly well to slow down, regain our equilibrium and get to know our new community and environment. We were sure everything would fall into place eventually. It is commonly said that after emigrating to a new country it can take up to five years to reach the standard of living that was left behind, and to fully find your feet. That is probably true, but we were never expecting to be in exactly the same situation as we were before we left South Africa. Our lives were irrevocably altered after losing Alex and William, so how could we ever regain what we had lost? Our family had paid a very high price in the stakes of life, and all we wanted out of the future was to have a relatively decent and comfortable life, and nothing more.

Having been a city dweller for most of my life, and very much enjoying city life, the change to a small island community was surprisingly easy. The friendly, close-knit community was very welcoming to us, and we immediately felt at home. We joined the pipe band within a week of my arrival, when Patrick was here for a few days, and a few months later we joined a Scottish country dancing group. Not that we were much good at the dancing side of it, we were rather hopeless at times with all the steps and routines, but we met new people, had a few good laughs, and we learned enough about country dancing to at least manage well enough at the local family ceilidhs, which are held in the summer months. The ceilidhs are a great part of the summer season, with all ages welcome, and it is not unusual to have a three- or four-year-old as a dancing partner at some point in the evening. It gets particularly enjoyable when there are visitors to the island during the summer months who know even less than we do about the different dances, and things can get quite entertaining, particularly when there are young people who have enjoyed more than their fair share of alcoholic refreshments and their energy levels are a bit much for the rest of us.

One night we were in the village hall at a little variety concert which was organised by the local drama club, and we found a form on the table inviting people to join the club. We thought it would be worth a try and so we filled in the form there and then. Unlike Patrick, who had taken part in amateur dramatics when he was younger, this was a new experience for me, but I suppose there is always something new in life worth trying out. My first part in our drama group was that of an old lady named Betty, who was in a care home for the elderly. She was quite a feisty character, much to the dismay of her selfish adult daughter, who resented the cost of the care home, because she saw it as a waste of her inheritance. The play starts quite upbeat and funny, but slowly turns rather dark and sinister, as the daughter plots against her mother. We made good friends during rehearsals and the run of the play, and Betty grew on me during that time. I rather missed the old dear when we were finished. We have had some fun moments in the drama club, and the weirdest part I have had is the part of one of the 'Lost Boys' in the Peter Pan pantomime. My particular 'lost boy' had clearly been lost for a very, very long time, in fact for many decades, because he was quite old! But to be fair, in the absence of available children for the parts, all the 'boys' were a bit past their prime, some rather more than others. Our drama group only rehearses once a week, on a Tuesday evening, and that rehearsal period lasts for about six or seven weeks, which means we end up having just six or seven rehearsals. It may sound as if that is not enough time, but everything works out perfectly well in the end. Everyone learns their lines, gets their costumes together, finds any props they may need, and then we have the sound technician and a lighting technician who come in a few days before opening night for a tech rehearsal. That's it, and away we go.

CHAPTER 32

A few months after his arrival Patrick started thinking about how to start a new career. He knew that to practice as an advocate in Scotland he would have to write several exams and satisfy many other stringent requirements, and then he would have to work on the mainland every day. This was not something he was overly enthusiastic about, but despite these reservations he decided to travel to Edinburgh after arranging a meeting at the Faculty of Advocates to find out more about the requirements, in case he decided to pursue that line anyway. Unfortunately he was met by a surly group of 'people in grey suits' who clearly had no interest in trying to encourage him in any way, and he returned home feeling somewhat demoralised by their negative attitude. He got the impression that they were doing everything they could to put him off, and they succeeded, because he was very much put off by their attitude. With that option not worth pursuing, Patrick turned his attention to possible opportunities in a career as a mediator, and he ultimately enrolled at the University of Strathclyde to do a Master's degree in mediation. The regular travelling to the mainland for lectures were a bit inconvenient, but he thoroughly enjoyed the course and after graduating he started on his new career path, which is now a very successful mediation practice, mostly via Zoom or teleconference, but occasionally in person when he travels to the mainland. Most importantly, he is thoroughly enjoying the new direction in which his career has taken him, and the 'surly people in grey suits' actually did him an immense favour by putting him off. As for myself, I picked up a handful of piano pupils which meant I could continue teaching, something I have always enjoyed. But we were still intent on buying a flat as a holiday let, although we didn't want to rush into it, so we just kept our eyes open for something suitable. The flat had to be close to our house, and without a garden, because a garden would need too much attention. Eventually the ideal flat came on the market, and we wasted no time putting in an offer. It is only five minutes away by car, and it is a perfect holiday flat which overlooks the Firth of Clyde, with the front door just a few steps away from the beach. The flat is usually fully booked from about April to October, and because we do all the admin, cleaning and laundry ourselves, it has been a good source of income. Not quite enough to make us rich, but definitely worth our while.

Although the flat is fully booked for about seven months of the year we get less bookings during the winter months, and during the 2020 and 2021 lockdowns and restrictions we took full advantage of that. The 2020 lockdown rules were particularly strict in Scotland with everything closed and everyone pretty much confined to their homes, even for Hogmanay. After a year of such irrational nonsense we were determined to 'go out for Hogmanay', so we decided to use our flat for our night out. We spent the afternoon in the flat preparing platters of lovely snacks, we stocked up on a few bottles of good wine including our own strawberry wine and elderflower wine, and Patrick, Catherine and I spent a most enjoyable evening 'out' for Hogmanay. As strange as it may sound, just being out of our own house was a real treat. It was the first time in almost twelve months that we were under a different roof, and it really felt as if we had gone somewhere special for a meal. The three of us had a true feast because Patrick and I had spared no effort in making the best food, and we opened excellent wine to celebrate the evening.

Just before midnight we went down to the small car park opposite our holiday flat, taking our bagpipes with us because we were determined to play 'Auld Lang Syne' at midnight, even if it was just for ourselves. The car park was deserted, the road was deserted, the houses surrounding the car park were in darkness, and the evening was completely silent. Hogmanay on Arran seemed to be well and truly cancelled. Everything was closed and eerily quiet as we stood in the car park waiting for Catherine to give us the signal that it was midnight, and at her signal Patrick and I started to play 'Auld Lang Syne' into the darkness. Within seconds lights were flicked on, people started leaning out of their windows or gathering on their balconies, and we could all once again feel the warmth of human contact, even if it was at a distance. As we finished playing someone called out, "Can you play some more please?" and naturally we obliged with a few more tunes. After the isolation of the preceding months I struggled to hold back my tears, because I knew that if I allowed myself to start crying I would probably not be able to stop. Just being in contact with other human beings was a very emotional experience. Our friends Tony and Ann-Marie, with their son Tom, had come down to the car park and because of the prevailing Covid rules, they kept their distance.

But after playing a few tunes on our pipes we invited them to join us outside our flat to toast the New Year. Yes, in the middle of the night and in the middle of a Scottish winter, we had to drink the toast outdoors, because overzealous scientists and politicians had decided that we were not allowed to meet indoors. But the prevailing insanity was not going to deter us, and we went through a good few bottles of our homemade strawberry wine and elderflower wine between the six of us, bringing in the New Year on a happy note.

One year later, at the end of 2021, these same scientists and politicians in Scotland decreed once more that Hogmanay across Scotland was cancelled, and we spent our evening in the flat again, but this time the rules were slightly relaxed and people were allowed to meet indoors in very limited numbers, so at least we could enjoy the company of our friends Tony and Ann-Marie again, and they brought friends with them, so we all had a wonderful evening together. I had posted on our local community Facebook page that we would be playing our pipes in the car park across the road at midnight, and we thought there would probably be a few hardy souls waiting for us to play 'Auld Lang Syne' at midnight. The weather was foul, and it was raining hard as we crossed the road to the car park, but much to our astonishment there was a crowd of at least thirty people huddled under their umbrellas waiting for us in the miserable weather!

We played 'Auld Lang Syne' at midnight, and then went on to play more tunes on the pipes, with a few people throwing caution to the wind by breaking the prevailing lockdown rules and dancing around in the rain. Everyone seemed to be happy and jolly, and it seemed to be an emotional release after the months of isolation and loneliness. Even standing in pouring rain, after midnight, in the middle of the winter, did not put them off because they very much wanted to share the moment with friends and neighbours. At one point a police van pulled up a short distance away and the police got out of the van to watch us. We were not sure if they were just bored and wanted to listen to the pipes, or if they had seen my post on Facebook about our plans to play in the car park and they wanted to make sure nobody forgot about that inhumane rule invented by scientists and politicians - social distancing. Whatever their reason for stopping, they kept at a distance and afterwards most of us called 'Happy New Year' to them, to which they replied in kind before getting into their van and driving off. I suppose it was not easy for them during those lockdown days, having to enforce rules that were so often totally random and pointless, and maybe all they wanted and needed was to celebrate the arrival of the New Year with others.

CHAPTER 33

Isle of Arran – July 2023

Six years have passed since I closed the front door behind us in Cricklewood, and Catherine and I set off on our long train and ferry journey from London to Arran. I have often been asked if I have any regrets about leaving South Africa and moving to Arran. To this I can honestly say that I have no regrets whatsoever, and I don't miss anything I used to have when I was still living in South Africa. It was easy for me to embrace a new life on the island, and the people of Arran welcomed us so warmly that it didn't take long for us to become a part of our community.

Something else we have also often been asked is *why* we came to Arran, and this question is much more difficult to answer honestly and simply. We usually just say we wanted a change, and we thought Arran was a good place to come to for a complete change. Sometimes that simple reply is enough, but more often than not, well-meaning people will want to know what made us choose Arran in particular, and then we need to go into more detail. Which means we have to explain about Alex, who worked on Arran in 2003 and had friends here who contacted me after he died, and the death of William, which prompted us to move here because we were hoping to build a new life. We don't mind sharing our story, because after all it has defined much of what we are now, but in a social setting we usually try and get away with the simple reply, and only expand on it when we are asked to. Despite our reservations, it has never caused any uncomfortable moments for us, just an acceptance of who and what we are.

The beautiful pink pebble I picked up on Brodick beach on that cold and windy January morning in 2015, after our brief visit to Arran to meet Alex's friends, still sits on a shelf next to my bed. That day I never thought we would ever come back to Arran, even for a visit.

But obviously the Universe had other plans for us.

ABOUT THE AUTHOR

Born and bred in South Africa, the author now lives on the Isle of Arran, off the West Coast of Scotland.
She shares her home with her husband, her daughter and her daughter's cat, two pet ducks, two parrots, an African dog, and three more cats, including two young and mischievous Siamese.
This is the second book by the author, with the first being the story of her great-great-grandmother, who was erased from the family history over one hundred years ago, but whose story was discovered by the author, and told in the book 'The Hidden Ancestor' (also available on Amazon).

Printed in Great Britain
by Amazon